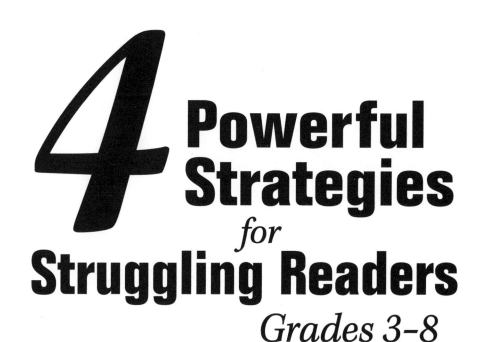

4 Powerful Strategies
for
Struggling Readers
Grades 3-8

Maurita,

What a pleasure it is to
meet a new concept-based
colleague dedicated to
literacy!
Best wishes in the
journey

4 Powerful Strategies
for Struggling Readers
Grades 3-8

Small Group Instruction
That Improves Comprehension

Lois A. Lanning

Foreword by Joseph Yukish

A Joint Publication

For information:

Corwin Press
A SAGE Company
2455 Teller Road
Thousand Oaks, California 91320
www.corwinpress.com

SAGE Ltd.
1 Oliver's Yard
55 City Road
London EC1Y 1SP
United Kingdom

SAGE India Pvt. Ltd.
B 1/I 1 Mohan Cooperative
    Industrial Area
Mathura Road, New Delhi 110 044
India

SAGE Asia-Pacific Pte. Ltd.
33 Pekin Street #02–01
Far East Square
Singapore 048763

International Reading Association
800 Barksdale Road
PO Box 8139
Newark, DE 19714-8139
www.reading.org

Printed in the United States of America.

Library of Congress Cataloging-in-Publication Data

Lanning, Lois A.
Four powerful strategies for struggling readers, grades 3–8: small group instruction that improves comprehension/Lois A. Lanning.
    p. cm.
Includes bibliographical references and index.
ISBN 978-1-4129-5726-7 (cloth: acid-free paper)
ISBN 978-1-4129-5727-4 (pbk.: acid-free paper)
IRA Stock Number: 9306
    1. Reading comprehension—Study and teaching (Elementary) 2. Reading comprehension. 3. Reading (Elementary) 4. Effective teaching. I. Title.

LB1050.45.L36 2009
372.47—dc22   008025494

This book is printed on acid-free paper.

08   09   10   11   12   10   9   8   7   6   5   4   3   2   1

Acquisitions Editor:	Cathy Hernandez
Editorial Assistant:	Ena Rosen
Production Editor:	Eric Garner
Copy Editor:	Gretchen Treadwell
Typesetter:	C&M Digitals (P) Ltd.
Proofreader:	Taryn Bigelow
Indexer:	Molly Hall
Cover Designer:	Monique Hahn

Contents

Foreword

Recently, while spending my time riding subways to and from Columbia University or to New York Public Schools reading a book in Erin Hunter's *Warriors* series, the excitement picked up when Bluestar, the Windclan leader of the group of wild cats, and two of her apprentices are attacked by rats. Bluestar is fatally injured and Firepaw, the orange tabby protagonist, is very concerned whether or not Bluestar is still alive. To his joy, Bluestar recovers, explaining that she lost the fourth life the Starclan Warriors (departed warrior cats whose spirits reside in a constellation) had given her. Later, when Bluestar confesses that she had actually lost her seventh life during the rat attack, Firepaw's anxiety rises again. This time he expresses his grave worry that the Windclan leader will leave them if two more fatal injuries occur.

In the second book of the series, Bluestar is stricken with "green cough" during the leaf bear (winter) season and loses an eighth life. Firepaw has been promoted from apprentice to warrior, and is now named Fireheart. He, as well as the other warriors, becomes very protective of Bluestar, refusing to allow her to participate in any other activities that place her in harm's way.

Although I have pulled only two scenarios from this totally mesmerizing series of books (mesmerizing especially if you, like me, are a cat lover), I use the previous paragraphs to illustrate my engagement with the book. In fact, I was so moved beyond merely reading the words that I missed several subway stops! I analyze my reading below.

I used information from my *background knowledge* (e.g., cats have nine lives) to *infer* that even though gravely ill, Bluestar could be revived. I *created meaningful connections* from my experiences of loyalty to school/university communities where I have taught and educational networks in which I have been a member, in order to understand the whole concept of honoring a "warrior code," holding the clan leader in a position of respect, having concerns about losing a leader.

I *inferred* from Fireheart's reaction that losing the fourth life was not good, but that Bluestar could still feel and function. To do this, I *drew conclusions* by using my knowledge of cats and several bits of text information: Only the help of Barkley allowed Bluestar to be freed from the gnawing rats; Bluestar was left with serious wounds; the warriors gathered spiderwebs to close the wounds; cats have nine lives, which left Bluestar with five; Bluestar opens her eyes and speaks to the waiting clan members; she is able to make the trip back to the Windclan Camp.

I *created meaningful connections* with my previous reading experiences with fantasy books (e.g., *Watership Down,* and my brief inquiry into mystics and new age thinking). I made *text-to-text connections* from these sources to help me understand the mystical qualities Hunter uses in her writing as she describes some of the environment, beliefs, artifacts, messages through dreams, and the setting of the warrior cats.

In all of my interactions with this text, I was *self-regulating,* using the sub-components (skills) of this and other strategies, to support my comprehension and create a realistic interpretation of Hunter's story. For example, I figured out that a road with moving vehicles is called a thunderpath.

My dialogue exemplifies a belief we must share about comprehension and comprehension instruction if we are to teach all children to become literate. James Flood and Diane Lapp (1991) ask educators to alter their belief that each text has one, true accurate meaning and accept what Rosenblatt (1978) calls "transaction" or interrogation between the text and the reader (p. 736). Therefore, to discuss my reading as I did, I had to bring as much to the page as the page brought to me.

The preceding discussion may not have been enough to get you to run out and buy a copy of the first book in the *Warriors* series, but one middle school child in New York City Public Schools did just that. He saw me in the school during my visit after I gave a book talk to his group about *Warriors: Into the Wild.* He excitedly walked up and said, "I got the book!!!" (Really his teacher went to the bookstore and bought it for him.)

We enjoyed a conversation about where he was in the first book, *Into the Wild,* where I was in the series, and our hopes and fears for Fireheart and the other members of the Windclan. The student was not able to use the italicized vocabulary that I used above to describe his reading. Nor did he realize that in order to fully comprehend Hunter's message and create an interpretation of her work, a reader may access one strategy and meld information and processing gleaned from several supporting skills while also integrating another strategy. But, I feel that this boy, if taught by a teacher who read, internalized, studied, and reshaped her teaching using Lois Lanning's book, *Four Powerful Strategies for Struggling Readers, Grades 3–8,* would be able to use some of the same language and behaviors I used to describe how he made sense of the struggles between the four clans of wild cats trying to survive in their territories that are being overtaken by "two-legs" (humans).

I have read and reread the chapters of *Four Powerful Strategies for Struggling Readers, Grades 3–8,* and through Lois Lanning's explanations, examples, and practical teaching recommendations, I can explain my comprehension processing using her terms. And, I do not feel I would have described my comprehension processing in the same way before reading her book. The first step in effective teaching requires us to have a thorough, research-based understanding of what we are trying to teach. We (teachers), like our students, benefit from the words of David Wood (1998): If children [teachers], (1) do not know what is relevant to the task as set, and (2) cannot analyze and grasp what they need to take into account, and if they are (3) unsure of the teacher's [comprehension teaching] motives, or if

(4) they assume that there is more to the problem than meets the eye, they will appear incompetent.

Lois makes us competent about the comprehension process and its most efficient strategies by citing numerous studies, papers, and authorities who are recognized as leaders in comprehension research. In addition, she has tested the words of these authorities by working with numerous groups of teachers and children implementing the theories that she built into her model of comprehension instruction. In her writing, Lois practices the research on transfer by using Bransford and Swartz's (1999) overriding principle of presenting new material: (1) in multiple contexts throughout the book, (2) through "what-if" problem solving for teaching comprehension strategies, and (3) by requiring us to invent solutions to a broad class of applications for teaching comprehension strategies rather than simply a teaching idea or graphic organizer to teach a single strategy.

Yes, I have heard the mantra from some teachers, "I don't want research, or theories, or models! I want practical ideas I can use tomorrow."

Through Lois's thorough, teacher-friendly descriptions of identified "best practices" in teaching comprehension, she gives examples of what this research means for effective teaching throughout her narrative. She follows this with practical descriptions of how to put these research ideas into practice in classroom situations. Her lesson examples are stellar and provide a road map for teachers to use in constructing other lessons around the skills and behaviors that lead to her Four Powerful Comprehension Strategies—*summarizing, creating meaningful connections, self-regulating, and inferring*—using a Gradual Release Lesson Model of strategy instruction.

I feel this book will become a major contribution to building an effective comprehension curriculum for struggling readers from Grades 3–8. But even further, the author herself challenges us to read many different sources, letting us know that this book will become one of a group of books that will assist us in moving toward effective teaching of comprehension to *all* children.

I would strongly encourage the readers of this book to read several of the books on teaching comprehension cited as well as others. Only by studying the literature can one begin to understand the complexities of comprehension. By reading widely and comparing authors' thinking, confusion and overlaps involving terminology become apparent (see p. 2 of this volume).

And I know this advice comes from Lois Lanning's heart, her own belief system, and her own practice. Lois and I have a history spanning many years. When she completed her master's degree in reading education at Ashland University, Ashland, Ohio, the faculty unanimously agreed that she should receive the "Outstanding Reading Educator Award." Her industry, quest for learning, willingness to challenge her thinking and the thinking of others, and her dedication to finding the best practices for helping all children learn earned her this award. As I watched her move from District Reading Consultant, to Principal of an elementary school, to Assistant Superintendent of Schools, and completion of her doctoral studies, this industry and quest for best teaching never ceased. She was and continues to be the administrator we dream of who understands teaching, studies with her teachers, and challenges herself and others to stretch their learning and mastery of teaching all children. She also found funds in budgets and grants to provide excellent staff development, which also provided instruction for students needing extra help in summer programs that continued through the school year.

In the late 1980s, Lois and I became colleagues when she moved to Connecticut and brought me in as a consultant to work with her teachers studying "Teaching for Integration of Sources of Information During Small Group Reading Instruction." As she moved from district to district, we continued to work together, watching children, teachers, and each other. We spent evenings in her home, eating the wonderful dinners cooked by her husband, Sam, boring him with our discoveries of the day. From this beginning work, we decided to branch out into her current studies and investigations of comprehension instruction for struggling students in upper elementary and middle school.

As she mentions in the Introduction, after a conversation at the very beginning of writing this book, our careers took us in different directions. Although we meet periodically at conferences, through e-mail, and during phone conversations, my current duties as Senior Primary Reading Advisor to the Columbia University Teachers College Reading and Writing Project prompted me to encourage Lois to write the book alone.

Reading the book in order to write this Foreword was an excellent opportunity for me to view the work she has done with her teachers over the past years, and marvel that she can still stretch my thinking through her written words. She will do that for you also as you work your way through these pages. Be prepared to dog-ear pages, use post-its, and insert your notes when you try something, but also be prepared to learn from a wonderful teacher, colleague, and dearest friend of mine.

—Joseph F. Yukish, PhD
Emeritus Professor of Education, Clemson University
Senior Primary Reading Advisor,
Teachers College Reading and Writing Project

Preface

The primary purpose of this book is to provide teachers of Grades 3–8 with a clear and concise picture of how to structure comprehension instruction for students who are not meeting grade level literacy standards. For teachers responsible for reading instruction in these grade levels, this book shares ideas for implementing the intensive, focused instruction necessary to accelerate students' reading progress. Because students who are not meeting grade level literacy standards often are also lagging in other subjects (where they are expected to be grade level readers), this book offers suggestions to content area teachers for leveraging students' literacy learning. The result can be life-changing when all teachers work together to improve a struggling reader's ability to comprehend text.

Why this book when there is so much written about reading comprehension? One answer is that within each author, research study, professional article, and book, lies a new chance to gain a new insight, another perspective, and/or confirmation of current practice. The complexities of the comprehension process and instruction are not yet fully understood so the writing must continue.

Chapter 1 consolidates much of the research-validated comprehension strategies others have written about and provides the rationale for the resulting Four Powerful Comprehension Strategies this book advocates explicitly teaching to struggling readers: *summarizing, creating meaningful connections, self-regulating,* and *inferring.* These strategies have "high utility" and transferability across all texts without overwhelming struggling readers. Focusing on four—rather than eight or ten or six—essential strategies, gives a struggling reader a tighter lens on the strategies and also the task of remembering is simplified. We know even average adults have a limited capacity to hold information in their working memories (George Miller's Classic Magical Number 7 +/– 2). The Four Powerful Strategies described in this book provide an economical and compelling way to organize and represent the essentials of comprehension. Additionally, many of the key skills embedded in these Four Powerful Strategies are identified so that teachers can help students learn how to organize their knowledge about comprehension without feeling besieged by a long list of discrete, disconnected performance expectations.

Chapter 1 concludes by examining what we know about the transfer of learning. Instruction of struggling readers needs to be carefully designed so that students are able to independently transfer their small group learning to other reading contexts. What we know about factors that support and/or inhibit the transfer of learning from one situation to another provides a rationale for using a Gradual Release Lesson Design (Duke & Pearson, 2002) when teaching struggling readers.

Chapter 2 reminds intermediate grade teachers that struggling readers need daily, explicit, small group instruction using a Gradual Release Lesson Design. By letting go of small group reading instruction too early, these students begin the downward spiral of school failure. This book argues that struggling readers in Grades 3–8 do not fully understand the comprehension process and therefore need explicit instruction and numerous experiences applying the strategies across many different types of text in order to discover the interconnectedness of strategic reading. As these students learn how to systematically control their strategy use to understand text, they begin to believe in themselves as readers and to transfer their reading strategies to other situations. We know that, ultimately, the key to successful reading comprehension is actively understanding the strategies and applying them in combination with other reading strategies to construct text meaning (Anderson, 1991). Proficient readers, unlike those who struggle, recognize the interplay among comprehension skills and strategies throughout the process of constructing text meaning.

The Four Powerful Comprehension Strategies are covered in Chapters 3 through 6, each of which contain two sample lessons for the strategy covered. These sample lessons show teachers how to structure instructional support as students learn how reading works. The lesson design shifts gradually from teacher control to student responsibility so that the teacher can be sure students are successful during their independent practice. Most of the sample lessons in this book are designed for small groups. The lessons describe effective instruction activities/techniques that support comprehension.

A lesson suggestion for content area teachers is also offered in each of the strategy chapters. It is important that content area teachers share the responsibility for helping the struggling reader. Content area lessons, designed to leverage literacy learning, not only provide support to struggling readers but help them learn the content material as well. When subject area instruction is organized around the important concepts of the discipline, the student is better able to make connections among the knowledge and facts being taught. If students know in advance what kinds of relationships to look for and are reminded to look for them while reading their content area text, they will find it easier to identify important relationships in the material they read.

Chapter 7 concludes by bringing together the ideas discussed throughout this book and by leaving the reader with final questions and reflections to consider when planning small group instruction for struggling readers. Chapter 7 is followed by the Glossary which provides in-depth definitions of the Four Powerful Strategies and other terminology. The Glossary is a critical piece to understanding the whole. It ensures that we, reader and author, share common definitions of terms. *Although each chapter includes key terminology explained by excerpts from the Glossary, I suggest reading the Glossary in its entirety as the best way to begin this book.*

Struggling readers are at the heart of my work as an educator. During my career as a special education teacher at all school levels, classroom teacher, and districtwide reading consultant, it became clear to me that the children who leave the primary grades still struggling with reading face a dismal school future. As these students enter middle school and high school, they become further marginalized by daunting textbooks with readabilities well beyond their reach, increased writing expectations, less small group instruction, and a more fragmented school schedule. My commitment to reaching these readers never waned when I moved into school administration. In fact, I believe the literacy work I continue to do with many talented teachers is what keeps me grounded in my current position.

Continuing to learn how to help struggling readers is one thing—writing a book about it is quite another! Almost a decade ago, after presenting at an International Reading Association Conference with my good friend and mentor, Dr. Joseph Yukish, we sat in a diner in Atlanta and talked about capturing some of our ideas and beliefs in a book. We both returned to our very busy lives but continued to stay in touch and nudge each other's thinking via e-mail and occasional visits. After extending my comprehension conversations with many Connecticut teachers (most recently with the wonderful literacy teachers in Pomperaug Regional School District 15, Middlebury/Southbury, Connecticut, and in an Interdistrict Summer School Program), my understanding of this work was pushed to a much deeper level. As teachers I worked with began to implement the practices advocated in this book, success stories began to emerge. Now I am taking the plunge and sharing these ideas with other educators whose obligation is to help struggling readers. It is my sincere hope that *Four Powerful Strategies for Struggling Readers, Grades 3–8* provides readers with at least a few new ideas and understandings about comprehension instruction.

Acknowledgments

My commitment to helping struggling readers began at the onset of my teaching career. It did not take long to realize how essential the collaboration of highly knowledgeable colleagues is to successfully reaching students who find reading an embarrassing, frustrating, and wearisome task. I continue to be richly blessed with numerous opportunities to grow and learn from many outstanding and talented educators.

In the preparation of this book, debts are owed to writers who influenced my thinking. P. David Pearson, Nell Duke, and Gerald Duffy are among those whose work I returned to again and again for guidance. Several friends and accomplished educators read and commented on the many drafts of my manuscript and their advice made each version better. The assistance and inspiration of my close friends, Joe Yukish and Lynn Erickson, helped me focus on the light at the end of this undertaking. The detailed feedback from exemplary teachers, Terri Thorndike, Michelle Dawson, Julie Luby, Bev Poulin, Laura Mead, Joanne Riback, Sarah Cable, and Neil Cummins was especially valuable. After sending off a draft, I could hardly wait to read their constructive suggestions, corrections, and comments in the margins cheering me on!

To my husband, Sam, I express my deepest gratitude. His patience with my messy office and willingness to take on more household chores enabled me to persist in this work well into the night.

PUBLISHER'S ACKNOWLEDGMENTS

Corwin Press gratefully acknowledges the contributions of the following reviewers:

Amy Broemmel
Assistant Professor
University of Tennessee
Knoxville, TN

David B. Cohen
English & Reading Teacher, Academic Advisor
Palo Alto High School
Palo Alto, CA

xvi FOUR POWERFUL STRATEGIES FOR STRUGGLING READERS, GRADES 3–8

Ellen E. Coulson
U.S. History Teacher
Sig Rogich Middle School
Las Vegas, NV

Carol Gallegos
Literacy Coach
Hanford Elementary School District
Hanford, CA

Marta Gardner
Elementary Literacy Content Expert
Los Angeles Unified School District
Los Angeles, CA

Jude A. Huntz
English and Writing Instructor
The Barstow School
Kansas City, MO

Gayla LeMay
History Teacher
Radloff Middle School
Duluth, GA

Robert D. Losee
Teacher
Alpine Elementary School
Columbus Public Schools
Columbus, OH

Natalie S. McAvoy
Reading Specialist
Elkhorn Area Schools
Elkhorn, WI

Victoria N. Seeger
Literacy Coach
Seaman Unified School District #345
Topeka, KS

About the Author

Lois A. Lanning is currently the Assistant Superintendent of Schools in Pomperaug Regional School District 15, Connecticut. In addition to being an assistant superintendent, other roles in her career include classroom teacher, K–12 reading consultant, special education teacher, elementary principal, district curriculum director, and adjunct professor. These positions span urban, suburban, and small town school systems, giving her a wide view of literacy practices.

Lois has extensive background in district-level curriculum work and staff development training. She stays actively involved in the trends and issues in reading instruction through professional organizations, by presenting at state and national conferences, and by working with other school districts and state departments. She is the author of several articles published in professional journals and of other reading resources for teachers. First and foremost, her passion is helping all students become lifelong readers.

1

Foundations

Some comprehension strategies are more effective than others. Teachers who are trained in these strategies can help their students achieve increased levels of comprehension.

—International Reading Association (2003)

KEY TERMINOLOGY

Reading Strategies: Sinatra, Brown, and Reynolds (2002) define strategies as goal-directed, cognitive operations over and above the processes that are a natural consequence of carrying out a task.

Reading Skills: Skills are the smaller operations or actions that are embedded in strategies and, when appropriately applied, they "allow" the strategies to deepen comprehension.

Text: The term text is used to describe any language event, oral, written, or visual, in any format.

RECENT FINDINGS FROM COMPREHENSION RESEARCH

The RAND Reading Study Group (RRSG) (2002) defines reading comprehension as the process of simultaneously *extracting* and *constructing* meaning. Translating print to sounds and words while simultaneously making meaning is a highly complex act that is often overwhelming for a struggling reader. RRSG confirmed what many of us have witnessed, "that some of the good third grade readers will progress on their own to proficiency in reading, but many will not. Many will need explicit, well-designed instruction in reading comprehension to continue to make progress" (p. 2).

As studies of comprehension continue, some strong parallels have surfaced across the findings. One consistent conclusion is that some comprehension strategies are more effective than others (Duke & Pearson, 2002; Harvey & Goudvis, 2000; Keene & Zimmermann, 1997; Pearson, Roehler, Dole, & Duffy, 1992; RRSG, 2002). Researchers have been able to identify strategies that represent the essence of reading comprehension by systematically investigating the reading strategies that proficient readers use to understand what they read (Harvey & Goudvis, 2000). Further, findings show that teachers who are trained in these strategies can help their students achieve increased levels of comprehension. What is important to remember is that over time and with appropriate instruction, most students are capable of learning to use effective reading strategies to increase their comprehension.

So what are the reading strategies that proficient readers use successfully and automatically? Different authors cite similar but distinct comprehension strategies as those most essential to reading. Some are included in this chapter as examples. I would strongly encourage the readers of this book to read several of the examples cited as well as others. Only by studying the literature can one begin to understand the complexities of comprehension. By reading widely and comparing authors' thinking, the differences and overlaps in the use of various terms become apparent. Some writers tend to coin terms that on the surface sound new and distinctive, but in fact describe the same skill under a different label by other sources.

After analyzing numerous resources on comprehension strategies, having extensive conversations with colleagues, and synthesizing the findings of our collective experiences in teaching comprehension strategies to children, the conviction emerged that the Four Powerful Comprehension Strategies advocated in this book are strategies worth teaching well and deeply:

- **summarizing**
- **creating meaningful connections**
- **self-regulating**
- **inferring**

Numerous authors have lists of essential comprehension strategies. One way to broaden your understanding of the comprehension process is to recognize which strategies you use as an effective reader, when you use them, and why they strengthen your comprehension (see Appendix 1 for such activities). Later, as you continue to read what other writers say are essential strategies, you can compare their findings with your experiences as a reader. This awareness will go a long way in helping you make good decisions about comprehension instruction in the classroom.

Since this book is intended to be more pragmatic than academic, only a sampling of the studies and articles that are integral in promoting the ideas in this book are presented:

"Developing Expertise in Reading Comprehension" by P. David Pearson, Laura R. Roehler, Janice A. Dole, and Gerald G. Duffy in *What Research Has to Say*

About Reading Instruction, Second Edition. S. Jay Samuels and Alan E. Farstrup, Editors. International Reading Association Publication, 1992.

Essential Comprehension Strategies:

- searching for connections between what one knows and the new information in text
- monitoring the adequacy of text meaning
- repairing faulty comprehension upon realization that understanding has broken down
- distinguishing important from less important ideas
- synthesizing information within and across texts and reading experiences
- drawing inferences during and after reading
- asking questions of oneself, the author, and the text

Invitations to Literacy by J. David Cooper, John J. Pikulski, Kathryn H. Au, Margarita Calderon, and Jacqueline C. Comas. Houghton Mifflin Publishers, 1997.

Essential Comprehension Strategies:

- inferring
- identifying important information
- monitoring
- summarizing
- generating questions

Strategies That Work by Stephanie Harvey and Anne Goudvis. Stenhouse Publishers, 2000.

Essential Comprehension Strategies:

- making connections between prior knowledge and text
- asking questions
- visualizing
- drawing inferences
- determining important ideas
- synthesizing information
- repairing understanding

What Really Matters for Struggling Readers: Designing Research-Based Programs by Richard L. Allington. Addison-Wesley Longman Publishers, 2001.

Essential Comprehension Strategies:

- activating prior knowledge to make connections
- summarizing
- including story grammar lessons
- applying imagery
- generating questions
- prompting thinking aloud

Reading for Understanding: Toward an R&D Program in Reading Comprehension, prepared for the U. S. Department of Education's Office of Educational Research and Improvement. RAND Publication, 2002.

Essential Comprehension Strategies:
- questioning
- summarizing
- monitoring comprehension
- using graphic organizers

Super 6 Comprehension Strategies by Lori Oczkus. Christopher-Gordon Publishers, 2004

Essential Comprehension Strategies:
- connecting
- predicting/inferring
- questioning
- monitoring
- summarizing/synthesizing

7 Strategies of Highly Effective Readers by Elaine McEwan. Corwin Press, 2004

Essential Comprehension Strategies:
- activating
- inferring
- monitoring/clarifying
- questioning
- searching/selecting
- summarizing
- visualizing/organizing

Why Four Powerful Strategies?

Several years ago, when my colleagues and I started talking about how things were going with our work teaching comprehension to struggling, intermediate grade readers, we focused our discussions on those strategies that represent the essence of what efficient readers use to construct meaning. We decided that a *less is more* philosophy is important since we recognized that struggling readers are often overwhelmed and easily confused with too much information. We wanted to help these students develop a *depth* of understanding of a few powerful, transferable strategies rather than have exposure to a *breadth* of strategies that become mind-boggling and disconnected. Duke and Pearson (2002) tell us it is now known that there are a number of effective comprehension strategies, but also suspect that there is a point of diminishing return . . . the field could continue to focus on identifying more effective strategies, but perhaps attention is better focused on refining and prioritizing the strategies we already know about. Researchers have discovered there are several strategies, called general reading processes, that readers use every time they read anything.

With these thoughts in mind, we began our journey of studying the strategies most commonly discussed in comprehension literature; we continued our rich conversations and debates; we made presentations to hundreds of teachers and solicited their thoughts and opinions; and slowly we began to come to consensus about how to best represent and discuss the strategies used by proficient readers. Our end result was the four comprehension strategies that we now place at the forefront of our work: *summarizing, creating meaningful connections, self-regulating,* and *inferring.* This chapter outlines the rationale for these strategies. They are also defined in the Glossary at the end of this book and are discussed in depth in chapters devoted to each. Before delving into the rationale for these four strategies, I would like to share a few personal experiences that occurred while working on this book that gave me the confidence that we were on the right track.

It was mid-fall and I was out visiting an elementary school. I stopped by a third grade classroom just as six, obviously eager, readers were called by the teacher to the back table. The classroom was print rich and well organized. It was obvious that the students had learned the teacher's management routines as they arrived at the table promptly, placed their materials down, took their seats, and earnestly turned their faces to the teacher. After a brief lesson introduction, the teacher handed each student a copy of the short book they would be reading. The teacher reminded the children that they would be reading orally at times and sometimes silently, and if they needed any reminders of the strategies good readers use, they could borrow one of the strategy rings placed in the center of the table. Now I was hooked. I had to stay for the remainder of the lesson.

When the teacher asked Amy if she would read the first paragraph aloud for the group, Amy enthusiastically began reading. At the end of the second paragraph she stopped. She studied the word "garage" while all the other students stared at the same word in their books. After a few seconds, Amy reached into the center of the table for the strategy ring. Held together by a large metal ring were nine strips of hole-punched tag paper. Each strip, approximately three inches wide and six inches long, had a different reading strategy written on it. Amy started flipping through the options. The group waited patiently, as did the teacher. When Amy began to fumble with the volume of strips, the teacher prompted, "Which strategy are you looking for, Amy?" Amy was now making her third trip around the strips. Amy was having difficulty deciding, she was becoming anxious, and her focus was getting farther and farther away from the text.

A similar experience occurred in another classroom a few weeks later. Students were scattered around this fifth grade room reading silently. They had a pencil and packets of small post-it notes close by. I sat down on the floor with one student and asked if he could talk with me about how he was using his post-it notes. "I'm writing a code on it that shows what I am thinking about while I read and then I'm sticking it in my book to mark the spot," he confidently answered. I noticed the four notes he had stuck in various spots of his book all had the same code written on them: T-S. This code, he explained, meant he made a text-to-self connection at that particular spot in his reading. "What other kinds of codes might you use?" I asked. He hesitated and then said he couldn't remember the other codes because there were a lot, but he would be glad to go get his code sheet from his desk and show me. After rummaging through his already jumbled desk for several minutes, he was delighted to retrieve the rumpled code sheet. We sat and looked at it together. There were approximately ten separate codes for various types of reading behaviors, some of which he could explain but some for which his response was, "I forget what that one means." (Contrast this use of post-it notes with how they are used in the first sample lesson in Chapter 4.)

These two scenarios struck me because the teachers in both classrooms are conscientious, hard-working educators trying to do what is best for their struggling readers. However, the menu of strategies they were asking students to use was mind-boggling—especially for the students whose comprehension is so fragile. Additionally, in interviewing the students, I found they frequently had a procedural knowledge of a few of the reading strategies and skills (e.g., they could retell the steps of a strategy), but they had difficulty explaining why the strategy was important or when it should be used during reading.

A limited inventory of strategies not only becomes more manageable for students, it provides instructional focus. This focus allows teachers to spend more time unpacking the complexities of the comprehension strategies and modeling their use across many different types of texts. With fewer strategies, students gain repeated opportunities to practice, discuss, and consequently develop a deeper understanding of each one and how they all support each other. Readers begin to independently transfer their learning of strategies to other reading situations. In other words, *less* truly can be *more*. These beliefs served as guidelines and strengthened the efforts my colleagues and I used to consolidate the growing volume of literature related to comprehension strategies into a meaningful, concise, and powerful few.

The Four Powerful Comprehension Strategies

Summarizing, creating meaningful connections, self-regulating, and *inferring* are not only acknowledged in this book but in many others as strategies essential to reading comprehension (Allington, 2001; Cooper, Pikulski, Au, Calderon, & Comas, 1997; Harvey & Goudvis, 2000; Keene & Zimmermann, 1997; Oczkus, 2004; RRSG, 2002). In this book, the most encompassing name is used to describe each strategy in order to best reflect all the skills that the strategy implies. For instance, this book uses the term *self-regulating* as an essential reading strategy to ensure comprehension is maintained; other writers use the term "monitoring." The cognitive skills involved when a reader is self-regulating include monitoring text meaning, but are broader. The strategy self-regulating also refers to readers solving problems when meaning breaks down, and being aware of how the reading situation will affect his or her understanding.

Some writers use strategy terms that are redundant or only shades apart in their distinction. For example, determining importance in text and finding main ideas are strategies defined in the same manner by different authors.

Writers' lists of essential comprehension strategies also differ in length. The Four Powerful Comprehension Strategies identify and synthesize the common threads running through the literature and identify the *skills* that support each strategy. Finally, the four strategy sets presented here are well supported across reading comprehension research.

One word of caution: There is an inherent problem in a list; it gives the impression that each item is accessed separately and is more or less important depending on its placement. People typically approach a list this way in their efforts to manage the items, but the more items there are, the more likely the illusion will persist that each strategy and skill has a separate identity and that one may be more essential than the other. This is yet another reason to keep things succinct and to the point!

Collapsing the comprehension work and thoughts of many resulted in a short inventory of four strategies with a listing of skills embedded under each strategy heading (see Figure 1.1). It is important to point out, again, the strategy and skill sets are highly interrelated but are not hierarchical in nature.

Strategy: Summarizing

Summarizing requires the reader to identify, paraphrase, and integrate important text information. Summarizing may occur across different lengths of text. For example, a reader may summarize across sentences, paragraphs, an entire passage, or across texts. Summarizing is one of the "Big Four" Strategies, as it requires a reader to sufficiently understand the intended message of the text in order to answer the question, "What is the author really saying?"

Summarizing is a strategy in which a reader is constantly synthesizing the important ideas in text. While summarizing, the reader determines what is important (main ideas), and eliminates redundant information and supporting details. Summaries are significantly shorter than the original text and take a broad overview of the source material. Summaries allow the reader to keep track of the ideas or opinions of the author without necessarily hanging on to all the supporting details.

In creating summaries of content material, a reader may organize the critical information of the text into generalizations or statements that represent a composite of the "big ideas" presented. Explicitly teaching students how the strategy summarizing may help them arrive at generalizations that represent important concepts and facts will facilitate deeper understanding. H. Lynn Erickson (2002) tells us that the process of designing and teaching a concept-based curriculum focuses on teaching toward the generalizations of the discipline that transfer across time and cultures. Can we strengthen this notion further by teaching readers how summarizing can help them independently recognize the important, enduring ideas? Erickson (2002) cites the work of Caine and Caine (1997), who discuss deep and felt meaning. We know that in order to move comprehension beyond the literal level and get to a deeper understanding of text, readers need to be more strategically engaged with their reading. Felt meaning takes a reader even further. Caine and Caine tell us, "It is an almost visceral sense of relationship, an unarticulated sense of connectedness that ultimately culminates in insight. . . . It is the coming together of

Figure 1.1 Four Powerful Comprehension Strategies

Summarizing	Creating Meaningful Connections

• Identifying important information (main idea)
• Distinguishing between a topic and main idea
• Generalizing important information & ideas (concepts)
• Determining and sequencing events and ideas
• Identifying genre
• Identifying type of text structure
• Categorizing and classifying using text information and background knowledge
• Paraphrasing
• Questioning: e.g., *How does this paragraph relate to the text information read so far? Which graphic organizer would I use to present the information in this selection? What essential points is the author making?*
• Synthesizing concepts and events
	• Imaging
	• Being aware of text language
	• Activating prior knowledge/experience:
	 ○ Previewing
	 ○ Making Text Connections:
	  — Text to Self (T-S) *Comparing and evaluating background experiences and images with information and descriptions presented*
	  — Text to Text (T-T) *Comparing and analyzing characters, plots, themes, information, purposes, descriptions, writing styles, and/or versions of texts*
	  — Text to World (T-W) *Comparing and considering text information with knowledge of the world*
	• Questioning: e.g., *How does this character's feelings compare to mine when I was in a similar situation? What images does the language create in my mind? How do my connections help me better understand?*
	• Synthesizing various types of connections and text

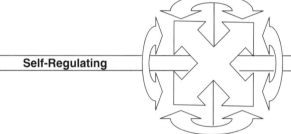

Self-Regulating	Inferring
• Knowing: self as a learner, the reading task, and reading strategies • Knowing the purpose for reading • Looking back, rereading and reading ahead • Predicting, confirming, clarifying, revising • Problem-solving words, phrases, or paragraphs • Cross checking multiple sources of information • Adjusting reading rate • Questioning: e.g., *What is going on in the text? Why am I reading this text? Are there ideas that don't fit together? Are there any words I don't understand? Is there information that doesn't agree with what I know? How can I problem solve to support my understanding?* • Synthesizing text with background info.	• Using background knowledge • Determining author's purpose • Being aware of text language • Recognizing author's biases/views • Making predictions • Determining theme • Drawing conclusions • Questioning: e.g., *What conclusion can I draw based on the ideas presented? What opinions are revealed in the selection? Where can I find clues about the character's feelings? What information is missing? Based on what I've read so far and what I know about this topic, what might come next? How can I use my questions to modify the emerging theme?* • Synthesizing text clues and various types of connections

SOURCE: © Yukish, Lanning, and England, 2001; revised by Lanning, 2005, 2007.

thoughts, and ideas and senses and impressions and emotions . . ." (as cited in Erickson, 2002, pp. 147–148). Summarizing, supported by other strategies, may be the key to reaching felt meaning.

Erickson's (2007) work in structuring curriculum around the essential generalizations of a discipline gives teachers clear ideas about which concepts to teach. A concept-based curriculum coupled with explicit instruction in complex performance process (e.g., summarizing) may help students learn how to independently unpack the important ideas in their content area reading. Summarizing is a cornerstone strategy for reading with understanding, for remembering what was read, and for transferring learning to new situations.

Teaching students to summarize what they read is a way to improve their overall comprehension of text. Dole, Duffy, Roehler, and Pearson (1991) describe summarizing as follows:

> Often confused with determining importance, summarizing is a broader, more synthetic activity for which determining importance is a necessary, but not sufficient, condition. The ability to summarize information requires readers to sift through large units of text, differentiate important from unimportant ideas, and then synthesize those ideas and create a new coherent text that stands for, by substantive criteria, the original. (p. 244)

Some authors (Harvey & Goudvis, 2000; Keene & Zimmermann, 1997) refer to "determining importance" as a major comprehension strategy. This book treats determining importance as a skill subsumed in the strategy summarizing. It is an important skill that a reader uses in creating a summary. There are a number of other important skills that are also embedded in this strategy and they are identified and discussed in Chapter 3, the Glossary, and Appendix 1.

Strategy: Creating Meaningful Connections

Readers make connections with text in a variety of ways. Connections with text are made by bringing one's background knowledge to the information in the text. When *creating meaningful connections*, a reader is relating his or her previous experiences, knowledge, and/or emotions to the ideas presented in the text. This important strategy has recently become overdone and misused in many classrooms. If the connections readers create are only at a surface level or focus on a minor detail from the text, the result is a shallow connection that does little or nothing to enhance the reader's comprehension. There are many skills in operation when a reader is creating meaningful connections.

Strategy: Self-Regulating

When *self-regulating*, a reader is continuously checking his or her reading to make sure it makes sense, and is also using a variety of "fix-up" skills when it does not make sense. Fountas and Pinnell (2001) point out that for developing readers this usually entails monitoring the language of the text. The focus of this book, however, is on struggling intermediate grade readers, and for them the process is more complex. As texts become longer in length, the content less familiar, the vocabulary load higher, and as authors employ more literary techniques in their writing, using the strategy of self-regulating not only becomes more critical to comprehension, but also demands more skills from the reader.

When meaning "breaks down," proficient readers know it and immediately begin to search for ways to recover meaning. For many struggling readers, this is the major problem. They may not become aware that they have departed from the meaning of the text until they are hopelessly confused or worse yet, until they have completed the text and been asked to respond. Jitendra, Hoppes, and Xin-Ping (2000) report that the effectiveness of self-regulating [instruction] for students with learning disabilities has been adequately demonstrated in numerous studies.

Self-regulating is one of the Four Powerful Comprehension Strategies because it is intricately embedded in the other three strategies: *summarizing, creating meaningful connections,* and *inferring.* Self-regulating is a systematic plan that a reader consciously adapts to improve individual performance.

Strategy: Inferring

Inferring is an essential reading strategy, as it not only facilitates comprehension but it also enhances the reader's enjoyment of text as new perspectives are discovered. It is a complex and sufficiently important strategy to warrant being considered one of the "Big Four."

One characteristic of skillful writing is an author's ability to tease the reader with subtle hints about how different story strands weave together to create intrigue and meaning. Readers search for insights and relationships among elements of text. They combine this information with their background experience and/or with other content to make predictions about where the text is going.

Readers infer differently depending on their purpose for reading. For example, inferences made while reading a nonfiction text for specific information may be based on the information supplied by the author. When readers are not familiar with a topic, they may need to rely on these text-based inferences in order to comprehend.

Inferences made while reading more familiar material or a narrative text for enjoyment may be more in the form of personal connections based on background knowledge and experiences (Durkin, 1993). There is a close relationship between the strategies *creating meaningful connections* and *inferring,* but as mentioned previously, an overreliance on personal connections while inferring may result in distorted comprehension (schema imposing) or may limit understanding to only that which is familiar. Readers need to constantly cross-check their inferences with other text information and utilize other skills that support inferring.

Summary of Recent Findings From Comprehension Research

What does this all say? Well, one message is that *less is more.* Research and writers have clearly identified a limited number of strategies that expert readers consistently use to ensure comprehension. Although there are shades of variation according to which author is being cited, the commonalities are strong. These may be considered the *power strategies* of reading. A reader must have many opportunities to consciously apply these strategies across different types of texts, must understand how and why each strategy facilitates comprehension, and must have years of reading practice in order to become a sophisticated, strategic reader.

While the strategies and skills in Figure 1.1 are in list form and addressed separately, the reader is reminded that the Four Powerful Strategies are processes that operate as a working *system* while reading. A reader uses them in an integrated and reciprocal manner before, during, and after reading. The integration of these reading processes results in efficient comprehension. This means that readers need to be proficient enough with each strategy so they can use them flexibly but deliberately, adapting them quickly and appropriately according to the demands of the text, the situation, and the reader's needs. These strategies have been shown to be important for all readers and should therefore be central to all reading curriculum and instruction.

In Chapters 3–6, these strategies are revisited, one at a time, with sample lesson plans designed to maximize the transfer of learning. The design and instructional activities of the lessons show how to effectively teach students the comprehension process by "unpacking" the skills embedded within each strategy.

KEY TERMINOLOGY

Instructional Activities/Techniques: Instructional activities are the means that teachers use to ensure that students become capable and confident comprehenders of text.

READING COMPREHENSION INSTRUCTION

The RAND Reading Study Group (RRSG) (2002) devoted a considerable amount of time and expertise to what we know about reading comprehension instruction and what we need to know. Some of their findings are very disturbing. For example, despite the well-developed knowledge base supporting the value of instruction designed to enhance comprehension, comprehension still receives inadequate instructional time and attention in most classrooms. Durkin (1978–1979) was the first to ring this alarm when, in her late 1970s studies of classroom reading instruction, she observed teachers devoted only 2 percent of their reading instruction to actually teaching children how to comprehend what they read. When comprehension instruction was present, many teachers appeared to be "mentioning" a skill to students and "assigning" it to them rather than employing the effective instruction, modeling, and transactional practices that research supports. RRSG went on to report that there is evidence that a relatively small set of strategies appears to be consistently effective across diverse populations of students, with diverse forms of text, and for diverse tasks that the reader is to accomplish (p. 46). Numerous studies show that when conscientious, diligent, and knowledgeable teachers apply strategy instruction in the classroom—even when applied imperfectly in the beginning—their students do improve in reading comprehension (NICHD, 2000, p. 48).

So what do the teachers who get these results do?

Comprehension Instructional Activities and Practices

We have precious little time left to help intermediate grade readers who continue to struggle, therefore we cannot afford to get sidetracked using creative activities that yield minimal results. We need to get the most out of our instructional practices and activities. Instructional activities are the vehicles teachers use to leverage students' strategy learning so they can better understand and interpret text. Some common instructional activities that relate specifically to reading comprehension include verbal and visual prompts; K-W-L; marking text (with sticky notes, check marks or comments in the margins, or highlighting); graphic organizers; vocabulary games; word sorts; Question-the-Author; Question-Answer-Relationship; Reciprocal Teaching; and so on. This is certainly not a full account of all the choices there are for instructional activities/techniques and you can already see why teachers become confused about what to do!

We want to select instructional activities and techniques that provide students with direct and relevant experiences in strategy learning and give them insight into what they are doing as readers to make meaning of text. In other words, the instructional activities we use need to clarify the teaching point (focus) of the lesson and the reading process. Some activities illustrate particular comprehension strategies better than others and may be more suited to students' needs and background experiences.

The instructional activity should be viewed as a *means* to facilitate students' deep understanding of strategies that support comprehension rather than as an end in itself. When asking students what they learned in their reading group on a given day, too often their replies refer to the teaching activities (e.g., "I learned how to sort sentence strips" or "I learned how to fill in a Venn diagram") rather than to the comprehension strategy under study (e.g., "I learned it is important to stop and reread when my reading no longer makes sense"). Instructional activities are highly familiar to teachers—"how to" books fill the shelves of teacher stores and are readily available online. But buyers beware; you cannot always judge a book by its cover! Many of these resources are jammed with worksheets and games that do not replicate authentic literacy experiences and may not give you the return on investment you expect.

What do authentic literacy activities look like? An article by Duke, Purcell-Gates, Hall, and Tower in *The Reading Teacher* (December 2006/January 2007) offers a definition so we can recognize authentic literacy when we see it. They suggest classroom literacy activities that represent a relevant purpose and utilize text that can be found in the lives of people outside of school. Here is an example of an authentic literacy activity: After closely observing the characteristics of goldfish as part of a science lab, *students* generate questions (based on the teacher's explicit minilesson of different types of questions). The students are then given time to search for answers in informational texts and on the Internet. Next, they return to the whole group to discuss and compare their information. Contrast this activity to one that is much less authentic: Students are directed to vocabulary words on the board, asked to write the words in their notebooks, and then look up the definition of each word in the glossary of their science textbook. Next, the students write the definitions in their notebook and turn in their papers at the end of class for grading. This is not a literacy activity we would find in the world beyond school.

It is recognized that some instructional activities are going to be for school purposes only because they are designed to assist in the explicit teaching of reading and writing. If the activities are too contrived, however, and students do not see them in use beyond the reading lesson, it makes the meaning and relevance of the learning less clear. If our goal is to teach for the transfer of the comprehension strategies and skills, we need to think carefully about how closely the instructional activities we use during a lesson and those that we assign for independent practice after the lesson reflect real-life purposes.

KEY TERMINOLOGY

Transfer: Broadly defined, transfer refers to the degree to which prior learning affects new learning or performance. A rich repertoire of teaching practices is necessary to facilitate transfer.

Research on the Transfer of Learning

Arguably, the transfer of learning is the ultimate goal of education. The most important skills, knowledge, attitudes, and understandings that students acquire through schooling are relevant because they have value and application in later times and in different circumstances. One of the most basic expectations of an educational school system is to ensure all students are literate so they are able to fully participate in our highly interactive, information society. One of the foundations of this book was to focus on the children whose transfer of learning, even after having four to six years of reading instruction, was negative (the learning from one context interferes in another) or was simply not achieved.

What Is Transfer?

As different theories of learning emerge, beliefs about the phenomenon of transfer reflect changes in the findings. Bigge and Shermis (1999) review several of the theories of learning that have most significantly influenced American education. For example, until the end of the nineteenth century, formal education was dominated by the doctrine of *mental discipline.* Those who subscribe to a conception of learning as a mental discipline generally believe the mind lies dormant until it is exercised. Schoolroom atmospheres under this theory of learning are recognized by an emphasis on memorization, lecture as a primary method of instruction, little connection between subjects, and challenging subject matter with long, difficult assignments. This theory adheres to the belief that transfer occurs automatically after content is covered because the mind has been disciplined. Wouldn't it be nice if it were that easy?

Perkins and Salomon (1988) call the expectation that transfer will automatically occur the "Bo Peep" theory of transfer: "Let them alone and they'll come home, wagging their tails behind them." Considerable research and everyday experience testify that it is inordinately optimistic to assume that transfer will take care of itself simply because material was covered or because instruction occurred. When conditions for transfer are met by chance, transfer may occur and " . . . the sheep come home by themselves. Otherwise, the sheep get lost" (Perkins & Salomon, p. 28).

B. F. Skinner's research proposed another theory of learning. He maintained behavior is learned through operant conditioning—response to (positive and negative) reinforcers—and thus, to Skinner's way of thinking, one's *repertoire* of conditioned operants is the basis for the transfer of one's learning. Skinner's theory requires teachers to develop a schedule of repeated reinforcements in order to maintain learning.

Newer theorists (cognitive interactionists) believe people interpret, not merely respond to stimuli . . . and that one's intentions and purposes motivate one's behavior (Bigge & Shermis, 1999, p. 230). In this view, learning is considered an insightful change in knowledge, skills, attitudes, values, and expectations, acquired through self-activated interactions. This theory of learning maintains that in order for learning to occur, what one is doing must be accompanied by either actual or modeled realization of the consequences. When transfer of learning occurs, it is evident in the form of the meanings, expectations, generalizations, concepts, or insights that were developed in one learning situation being employed in another.

A Closer Look at Transfer Theory

When discussing transfer, Perkins and Salomon (1988) talk about an individual's learning traveling to a new context in terms of "near and far" transfer. When problems and tasks are so much alike that the transfer of learning occurs fairly readily, it is considered *near transfer.* For example, the skills of driving a car quickly transfer to driving an unfamiliar truck. *Far transfer* refers to the attempt to transfer learning from one context to another when the sense of connection between the two learning situations requires deeper thinking, knowledge, and careful analysis. An example here may be using one's knowledge of how electrical systems work to facilitate an understanding of the network of arteries and veins in the circulatory system.

Perkins and Salomon (1988) expanded the "near and far" theory of transfer giving it more relevance to teaching. They apply near and far transfer to what they call a "low-road/high-road" model. "*Low-road transfer* reflects the automatic triggering of well-practiced routines in circumstances where there are considerable perceptual similarities to the original learning" (p. 25). In the example mentioned above, there is a great deal of resemblance between car and truck cabs so it would be considered an example of low-road transfer. To accomplish low-road transfer, a great deal of practice is necessary. Shoe tying, keyboarding, reciting sight words, or basic arithmetic facts are examples of low-road transfer tasks. A high level of automaticity (fluent processing) can be achieved with each of these tasks that is very useful. Thus, the closer literacy activities in school resemble the literacy expectations students will encounter outside of school, the probability that the school learning will transfer is increased.

High-road transfer is very different. High-road transfer depends on deliberate, mindful abstraction of skill or knowledge from one context for application to another. Such transfer is not generally spontaneous. It demands time and mental effort. High-road transfer always involves reflective thought in abstracting from one context and seeking connections with others (Perkins & Salomon, 1998, pp. 25–26).

Transfer is typically not as problematic in schooling when low-road transfer is involved. An illustration of low-road transfer in learning to read is to learn to decode words with automaticity. We see a lot of low-road transfer expectations in multiple choice tests and workbook tasks. A student may easily complete a worksheet matching vocabulary words in one column to definitions in another, but this same student may have difficulty comprehending the vocabulary in the context of his or her textbook where high-road transfer is needed.

Carefully planning our reading lessons to support the transfer of learning is especially important if we are going to reach our struggling readers. "Where transfer is typically more problematic is in the higher skills of *reading comprehension* [italics added], composition, math problem solving. . . . Furthermore, transfer is usually poorest with students who need it the most—with learning disabled students in the case of reading strategies" (Bereiter, 1995, pp. 26–28). This book supports teachers' ability to help struggling readers achieve the high-road transfer necessary in comprehension through (1) a gradual release lesson design (Chapter 2), (2) deep instruction in a few powerful reading strategies essential to comprehension, and (3) instructional activities that help illuminate how those strategies work to support comprehension.

Summary of Reading Comprehension Instruction

"Despite the significant body of research in the 1980s suggesting the effectiveness of strategy instruction, especially for low-achieving readers, strategy instruction has not been implemented in many American classrooms" (Dole, 2000, p. 62). Many reading programs still advocate teaching discrete skills apart from the coherent strategies that students need to become strategic readers. In planning a lesson, it is important to select instructional activities that clearly show students how reading strategies help them better understand text rather than activities that may overshadow the lesson point. It is too easy for struggling readers to miss the purpose with activities that do not closely represent the expected learning or do not represent authentic literacy.

Significant research maintains that the transfer of learning occurs when there is an understanding of the principles or generalizations of the learning task—in other words, the statements of relationships that represent many problems or experiences (Bigge & Shermis, 1999; Bransford, Brown, & Cocking, 2000; McKeough, Lupart, & Marini, 1995). When comprehension skills are bundled into broad strategies and deliberately mediated through instruction, across a variety of texts, we can do more to facilitate the high-road transfer of reading comprehension for those students who are struggling to make meaning of what they read. Four major comprehension strategies—*summarizing, creating meaningful connections, self-regulating,* and *inferring*—give purpose and relevance to the skills that support them and allow teachers and students to focus deeply on them in instruction over time. When students understand these broad strategies, the transfer of learning is more apt to occur.

The significance of teaching to the ideas in this book is just beginning to be demonstrated in the success of the readers whose teachers are using the ideas and instructional practices as presented. Chapter 2 now outlines a Gradual Release Lesson Design that is an important component of moving theory to practice.

2

Gradual Release to Accelerate Progress

Example is not the main thing in influencing others. It is the only thing.

—Albert Schweitzer (as cited in Anderson, 1975)

Think back to a complex, challenging learning experience that left you feeling proud and confident in your accomplishment. Was the experience connected to a sport? An academic class? A hobby? Think about the process you went through (the various stages of learning) and the levels of knowledge you needed to have in order to learn the complex task. Now think about how your performance improved with each phase of your learning. For example, let's think of someone learning to play golf. To play golf well, there are many components and layers of learning. A few are listed below to illustrate the point.

Factual knowledge—One needs to learn the goals, names, and use of different golf clubs, the basic rules, etiquette, and so on.

Conceptual knowledge—One needs an understanding of the key concepts that will determine how one plays the game such as the lay of the land (course), wind velocity, mental focus, motivation, and so on.

Strategies—One needs mental plans of what it takes to get the ball from here to there for various situations and conditions.

Skills—One needs an ability to adjust the golf swing and flight of the ball to effectively support the targeted strategy.

Obviously, learning golf is much more than swinging a club and hitting a ball. Like many other complex tasks, to become a good golfer, most people need quality instruction with specific feedback and many opportunities to practice on different types of golf courses. The progression from one stage of learning to the next is accelerated when closely guided by a teacher who understands the learner and the learning that needs to take place. The effective teacher is gradually releasing responsibility to the student to ensure sustainable progress and success.

How does this fit in with teaching struggling readers? Bigge and Shermis (1999) tell us that the critical question in regard to transfer (of learning) is what *conditions* engender the greatest amount of transfer. For example, teaching for transfer involves a lesson design that ensures students get explicit, focused instruction around a powerful teaching point that they will practice independently by the end of the lesson. There are several books on the market that explain how teachers in Grades 3–8 can structure and manage small group reading instruction in their classrooms. If intermediate grade teachers do make small group reading instruction a daily part of their work with struggling readers, too often the day to day teaching points are disconnected, do not follow a Gradual Release Lesson Design, and/or do not allow guided practice across a variety of types of text. As a result, many struggling readers never fully reach a deep understanding of how the comprehension process works.

Using a Gradual Release Lesson Design as a means to deliver focused comprehension instruction (around the Four Powerful Comprehension Strategies) can help deepen students' understanding and support the transfer of learning. Additionally, to help accelerate the learning of readers who lag behind, we need to provide practice with a variety of texts and appropriate scaffolding in a rich literacy community combined with a gradual release of responsibility from teacher to student.

GRADUAL RELEASE LESSON DESIGN

The teacher's role in instructing students is to maximize the likelihood that students will transfer their learning to new contexts independently. The five step *lesson procedure,* or Gradual Release Lesson Design, is patterned to scaffold the effective teaching of strategies in order to maximize transfer of students' learning. These steps are well researched (Duke & Pearson, 2002) and are used as a template for the small group reading lessons included at the end of each strategy chapter in this book. The steps are explained below.

1. **An explicit description of the strategy and how, when, where, and why to use it.** First, the teacher takes responsibility for succinctly and clearly explaining the strategy and skill that will be the teaching point of the lesson and linking it to the process of comprehension. The teacher is specifically focusing the students' attention on what they are going to do in the lesson. The teacher controls the discussion at this point but may invite students to participate by asking very explicit questions that further clarify the teaching point.

2. **Teacher and/or student modeling of the strategy in action.** The teacher is still in control at this step of the lesson. The particular teaching point of the lesson is demonstrated. The teacher makes his/her thinking public to reveal the strategic processing a good reader uses while comprehending text; "Watch how I do it."

   We don't want to assume a struggling reader will figure out what the teaching point of the lesson is about. Steps 1 and 2 may take 5 to 10 minutes of a 30-minute lesson. As subsequent lessons continue and student performance improves, these first steps are shortened to allow more time for student practice and engagement with text.

3. **Collaborative use of the strategy in action.** Students are now ready to begin putting the strategy into practice. The teacher is still leading the way but inviting students to try out the teaching point of the lesson; "You help me" or "Let's do this together."

   This small step precedes guided practice so the teacher can make sure students understand what is expected and can adjust any scaffolding that may be needed. We do not want struggling readers practicing strategies and skills incorrectly.

4. **Guided practice using the strategy with gradual release of responsibility.** Now students are ready to take over the work but still have the teacher close by with some assistance and feedback. The teacher closely observes student practice and, as needed, offers suggestions, nudging, and confirmation, but the teacher is increasingly pulling back and turning responsibility over to the students. This is a critical phase of the lesson. Decisions need to be made about how capable the students are to put the strategy into use independently. Before students are sent off to work without the teacher watching over them, they need to have enough guided practice to demonstrate their ability to be successful with the teaching point of the lesson.

   Ultimately, our goal is to help students realize what support they need to construct their own meaning of text. During this step, interaction is not limited to only one student and the teacher; rather, student to student discussion and support create a stronger sense of shared responsibility and deepens understanding.

5. **Independent use of the strategy.** Students are now ready to use the strategies and skills they have learned, often by themselves or with peers, because they have demonstrated a level of comfort and an ability to succeed independently. The type of task they are expected to perform needs to extend and reinforce the lesson. If students leave the small group only to go back to their seats and complete worksheets that are not authentic and well aligned with the lesson, the release of responsibility to the student is short-changed, the transfer of learning diminished, and the goal of accelerating progress weakened. Step 5 does not need to be a burden to lesson planning. Authentic reading and writing tasks (see Chapter 1) and peer discussion that encourage reflection on the comprehension process are highly effective activities.

The order of these steps reflects a gradual release of responsibility from teacher to students. The lesson procedures are conceptualized in Figure 2.1 below from Pearson and Gallagher's (1983) work on comprehension instruction.

Figure 2.1   Gradual Release of Responsibility Model

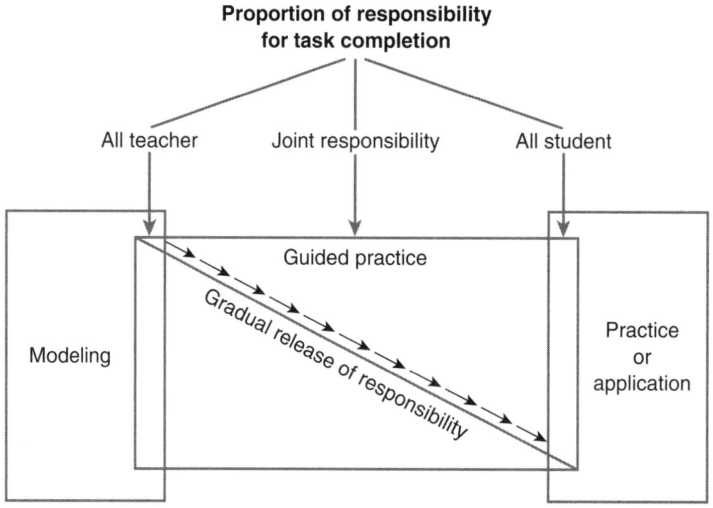

SOURCE: This figure was published in *Contemporary Educational Psychology*, Volume 8, Issue 3, P. David Pearson and Margaret C. Gallagher, "The Instruction of Reading Comprehension," Page 337, Academic Press (1983).

Using each of the five steps in every small group reading lesson is important for a few reasons: (1) The teacher is able to closely monitor students' progress in the lesson. If confusions arise, adjustments in instruction can occur quickly. (2) Students learn to know what to expect. Routines are especially important to students who are confused and lagging behind. Often the "locus of control" of struggling readers is outside of themselves, which means that rather than focusing their attention on their learning, they often spend more energy trying to figure out how to avoid looking foolish, guessing what the teacher expects from them, and what the "activity of the day" is now.

The mediated support of the Gradual Release Lesson Design offers struggling readers a chance to develop a deep understanding of the essential reading strategies that will help them make sense of text. High-road transfer of learning to other situations can be enhanced to a much greater degree for struggling readers through the bridging provided by using the five steps. "Bridging" means teaching so as to better meet the conditions for high-road transfer (Chapter 1). Rather than expecting students to achieve transfer spontaneously, the teacher "mediates the needed processes of abstraction and connection making" (Perkins & Salomon, 1988, p. 28). This involves teaching that gets students to make conscious abstractions and identify alternative applications of instructional material (James, 2006, p. 152).

Giving struggling students the opportunity to apply the lesson points across a variety of text genres that subtly increase in complexity of structure, length, vocabulary, concept load, and so on, is also important to building transfer and thus the acceleration of learning. For example, the teaching point of a lesson focusing on the strategy *creating meaningful connections* is the skill "text-to-text connections." During step 2 of her lesson (Modeling), see how the third grade teacher below helps students *bridge* the skill to a familiar text through her think-aloud:

> As I am reading this book *The Rough-Face Girl*, I am noticing that it has some things in common with the book *Cinderella*. I just learned both girls had mean sisters. Both Cinderella and the Rough-Face Girl had a hard life. They were very kindhearted people. . . . By thinking about these text-to-text connections, how the books are the same and how they are different, I now better understand both books.

In addition to the lesson procedures setting the conditions for transfer, instructional activities should be shaped so that they most closely "hug" the transfer desired. Hugging, which addresses low-road transfer, involves designing activities so they are similar to situations in which learners can apply what they have been taught (James, 2006, p. 152). For example, at the early stage of learning a new strategy, the lesson texts and activities should closely parallel (hug) the teaching point of the lesson making the skill and strategy very obvious to the struggling reader. The teaching point of the third grade lesson below is "determining and sequencing events and ideas," which is part of the strategy *summarizing*. The text closely "hugs" the teaching point by using transition words the students just discussed the previous day.

Teacher: We learned that authors often give us clue words to help us know that an event has changed. Do you remember some of the clue words we discussed?

Student: (looks at chart) First, second, next, last, finally.

Teacher: Exactly. As a warm-up, let's read this short paragraph and determine the sequence of events. Once we identify and sequence the events, we will be able to use this information to help us summarize our reading. "The New London City Zoo just received its first three animals. The first animal it received was a deer. The second animal it received was a monkey. The third animal it received was a lion. Children in New London are excited about the opening of the zoo!"

Using each of the steps of the Gradual Release Lesson Procedure balances explicit instruction with guided support to assist the transfer of learning. The steps of the lesson are used consistently yet flexibly so they follow the reader's responses thus preventing this design from being perceived as dogmatic. To accomplish this, the amount of time spent on each step is adjusted as more or less scaffolding is needed according to the reader's progress, familiarity with the text, and the learning situation.

The concept of scaffolding is grounded in the work of Lev Vygotsky (1978). Scaffolding refers to the structures that are put into place to enable a learner to carry out a task or solve a problem that is beyond his unassisted reach. If there is too much scaffolding, the opportunity to learn suffers and the inclination to defer the work to the teacher or more capable peer increases. If scaffolding is too weak, the learning becomes frustrating and exhausting as energy is overly spent on discrete parts of the task without understanding the goal.

There are six distinguishing features of scaffolding instruction (Meyer, 1993). As you read them, I think you will begin to see the rationale behind the five steps of the Gradual Release Lesson Design. Scaffolding features include

1. Teacher support that helps students relate new information to their prior knowledge

2. Transfer of responsibility from the teacher to the students

3. Dialogue that breaks from the traditional classroom discourse to more student-initiated talk

4. Nonevaluative collaboration that focuses on the student's potential for new learning rather than evaluating the student's current competencies

5. Appropriateness of the instructional level defined as what a student can do with assistance within his/her zone of proximal development

6. Coparticipation that creates opportunities for students to participate actively and cooperate in directing instruction

The process of the gradual release of responsibility from the teacher to the students (Pearson & Gallagher, 1983) is inherent in the features of scaffolding since the purpose of scaffolding instruction is to enable students to accomplish a task on their own, which initially they could not do without assistance. Mediating students' learning in this manner not only enhances their learning but also enables students to retain the learning longer and to be more flexible in transferring it to other situations (Kong, 2002).

Finally, to strengthen understanding, the Four Powerful Comprehension Strategies and skills taught through this Gradual Release Lesson Design need to be presented through multiple types of text and through "what if" problem solving. By carefully and deliberately teaching children to be mindful of their use of comprehension strategies across a broad variety of text examples, we can truly break the cycle of failure!

CONCLUSIONS AND REFLECTIONS

Teachers help students learn to comprehend well by

- explaining fully what the strategy and skill is that they are teaching and why, how, and when proficient readers use the strategy and skill while comprehending
- modeling their own thinking processes

- encouraging students to ask questions and discuss possible answers among themselves
- keeping students engaged in their reading via providing tasks that demand active involvement (RAND Reading Study Group, 2002)

Each of these actions is embedded in the lesson procedure outlined for comprehension strategy instruction. In addition, the steps of the lesson procedure support transfer theory, and when coupled with the appropriate teaching techniques, provide students—those who have difficulty comprehending—with the guidance they need to become independent, strategic readers. The lessons in this book are intended to follow a Gradual Release Lesson Design over time so that students deeply understand comprehension strategies and the transfer of learning is maximized. Recent research on how people learn shows that learning must occur with *understanding* if it is to be retained and transferred to new contexts (Bransford, Brown, & Cocking, 2000).

By honing down the list of reading strategies found in the literature and by identifying those strategies that require a reader to be mindful (to use conscious reasoning and planning while comprehending text), reading becomes a less daunting task for the reluctant, struggling reader. By identifying and teaching the "Big Four" Strategies and using them to organize and give purpose and relevance to the skills that support them, high-road transfer is promoted for the students who need it most.

Reflection Questions for the Reader

What are some of the ways your instruction currently supports the transfer of learning? How might you redesign your lessons for your struggling readers to ensure there is a gradual release of responsibility?

Which instructional activities closely "bridge" and/or "hug" the teaching points of your lesson?

How can you make sure that step 5 of the Gradual Release Lesson Design does not get dropped?

How can you encourage more student-to-student discourse in your small group lessons? How is increased student-to-student discourse an example of the gradual release of responsibility?

The next four chapters look at the instruction of each of the Four Powerful Comprehension Strategies: *summarizing, creating meaningful connections, self-regulating,* and *inferring.* Additional explanations are in the Glossary at the end of the book. Let's get started!

3

Putting the Strategies Into Practice

Summarizing

Knowing where you have been and where you are is a great benefit to knowing where you are going.

—Jeff Zwiers (2004)

The strategy *summarizing* requires a reader to be intensely involved with text. This strategy demands continual shifts of focus from the meaning of parts of text to how the parts relate to the evolving whole. Unlike casually skimming reading material, summarizing requires a reader to be deeply engaged with text, change gears (thoughts) flexibly, and integrate a variety of skills. When we talk with others about the books we have read, news we have heard, movies we have seen, or experiences we have had, we are summarizing . . . unless we are told, "Could you please get to the point!"

Summarizing is an essential strategy for students as they advance in grade levels and encounter longer length texts that they are expected to read independently. In summarizing, we are thinking about—almost unconsciously— text structure, vocabulary, and theme, which is why it is important we explicitly teach the struggling reader who does not understand the many skills that lie at the heart of the summarizing strategy.

KEY TERMINOLOGY

Summarizing: This strategy involves representing, in a few sentences and in your own words, the most important ideas of a longer passage or selection.

- **Identifying important information (main idea):** This skill requires one to distinguish the core concepts in a selection (that will be included in the summary) from the supporting or minor information (that will not be included in the summary).
- **Distinguishing between a topic and a main idea:** A topic is the general subject dealt with in a text or discussion. A main idea is the important thought (implied or expressed) that the author is conveying about the topic.
- **Identifying and generalizing important information and ideas (concepts), explicit and implicit:** A generalization is a broad statement that describes the relationship of two or more concepts (or main ideas).
- **Sequencing events and ideas:** Constructing summaries requires readers to track, order, and restate events described in the material being read.
- **Identifying genre:** Genres are categories or classifications of text formed by sets of conventions.
- **Identifying type of text structure:** How is the information organized? Authors make decisions about how to present information to readers depending on the type of text. Some structures are more representative of specific genres (fiction and nonfiction) and may use specific features (bold headings) to support the text structure.
- **Categorizing and classifying using text information and background knowledge:** This skill requires one to sort and organize information (especially in longer selections).
- **Paraphrasing:** Paraphrasing is restating or explaining ideas in your own words while retaining the meaning and ideas in the original selection.
- **Questioning:** Questions that support the strategy summarizing include: *How does this paragraph relate to the text information read so far? Which graphic organizer would I use to present the information in this selection? What essential points is the author making?*
- **Synthesizing information and concepts within text:** Synthesizing is putting parts (ideas) together into a unified whole.

WHAT IS SUMMARIZING?

As you can see, summarizing is a complex strategy that involves the orchestration of a variety of skills. While summarizing, a reader reduces large sections of text to the most important information. A summary, like a paraphrase, is a variation of an original passage in one's own words. Paraphrasing is the reworking of an author's word choice, sentence structure, or phrasing and is a skill essential to the strategy summarizing. A summary incorporates a broad overview of text and may describe common knowledge of a topic from several sources or may determine the important information of a single source.

This distilling down of longer length text to the points that are worth noting improves memory of what was read and strengthens comprehension. Summarizing requires readers to sift through the extra verbiage and/or extraneous details that an author may include in order to expand the ideas presented in the text. Often summarizing is defined as finding the main idea. Pearson et al. (1992) decline to use the term "main idea" opting instead to use the phrase "determining importance." They maintain that finding the main idea is merely one way to determine what is important. In this book, I take a fairly inclusive view of summarizing that incorporates terminology used by other authors. Identifying and generalizing important information and ideas is considered one of the essential skills that support the summarizing strategy.

Authors such as Fountas and Pinnell (2001) make a distinction between summarizing and synthesizing information from text. They define summarizing as being able "to present the substance or general idea in brief form," and synthesizing as being able "to bring together parts or elements to form a whole." Although they give the same reasons for why a reader needs to use each strategy, and how teachers can help readers learn each strategy, they distinguish synthesizing as the integration of the readers' background knowledge to arrive at a new understanding. Fountas and Pinnell define synthesizing as a skill that good readers use across *each* of the comprehension strategies. I agree with this line of thought about synthesizing so, in the Four Powerful Comprehension Strategies, you will see synthesis listed as a skill that enhances each of the Four Powerful Comprehension Strategies in subtly different ways.

In collapsing many comprehension systems down to the essential strategies described in this book, it made sense to consider synthesizing as a skill that supports the summarizing strategy. Indeed, synthesizing information is a logical extension of determining what's important in text while reading. Readers actually need to synthesize information across sections of text, or between texts, in order to create summaries (Pearson et al., 1992). This book's definition of summarizing is in keeping with Dole et al. (1991) who explain the strategy below:

> Often confused with determining importance, summarizing is a broader, more synthetic activity of which determining importance is a necessary, but not sufficient, condition. The ability to summarize information requires readers to sift through large units of text, differentiate important from unimportant ideas, and then synthesize those ideas and create a new coherent text that stands for, by substantive criteria, the original. This sounds difficult, and the research demonstrates that in fact, it is. (p. 244)

There are other authors (Harvey & Goudvis, 2000; Keene & Zimmermann, 1997) who refer to determining importance as a major comprehension strategy. As mentioned previously, this book considers determining importance a smaller skill that is included in the broader strategy of summarizing. By reviewing the list of skills embedded in this strategy, it should become clear why young readers often find summarizing a challenging process, and why this strategy extends beyond just locating important information. Summarizing is identified as one of the Four Powerful Strategies because as students learn how to closely analyze text for important information, their reading comprehension improves and they better understand what it takes to organize their writing.

WHEN DOES A READER SUMMARIZE?

When the text becomes longer or contains multiple ideas, a reader begins to call upon the strategy of summarizing in order to sustain and deepen comprehension. Often a reader begins summarizing at the individual paragraph level. As reading continues, the reader connects, revises, and extends the summary by creating a "summary of the summaries." Summarizing allows readers to engage in an ongoing interpretation of the text and to expand their comprehension as they continue to process text.

When you ask students to summarize, what usually happens? My experience shows the following for students who either have not acquired the skill or who are struggling readers: (1) they don't write enough, (2) they copy word-for-word from the text, (3) they miss the important information while trying to recall all the nonessential details and (4) they begin with an idea presented by the author then allow their own background knowledge to reinvent and override the text.

What should students do when asked to summarize? They should do what a competent reader does when using summarizing as a reading strategy. A competent reader summarizes in order to sort out what is important from the nonessential, redundant, and supporting information. Breaking down text to main ideas, connecting the ideas, and synthesizing them into larger ideas, are all skills embedded in the strategy summarizing. Additionally, noticing text structure allows the reader to see how the author organized and related ideas. A summary should follow the same text structure as the text being summarized. Finally, when a reader raises questions about what the author is really saying, he or she is gathering information to help with summarizing.

WHY DO READERS SUMMARIZE?

Summarizing is a strategy necessary for understanding both the literal and the implied meaning of text. Our working memories cannot hang on to massive amounts of disconnected information. Summarizing increases the retention of what was read by focusing the reader on the most important information. Why do we summarize? Jeff Zwiers (2004) says the main reason is brain capacity. He uses a great example of how we tend to group several related pieces of information together into one category once we hit the limit of our capacity to remember—for the average adult person that is approximately seven bits of information. (Another reason why Four Powerful Comprehension Strategies are enough for a struggling reader to remember!)

Summarizing is an especially important strategy to be explicitly taught to readers with weak comprehension. These students get lost trying to follow an author's line of argument and in articles that are stuffed with facts—especially if the information is unfamiliar! Since a significant amount of reading in the twenty-first century is nonfiction—technical or informational—and is received rapid-fire via the Internet, readers who cannot summarize efficiently (that is, digest and extrapolate main points from large passages of text) will quickly fall further and further behind.

While working their way through text constructing and revising summaries, readers are in effect creating an interdependent cycle of connected summaries. As summaries build on each other, readers become more deeply engaged in their reading and can make better decisions about what is important. The struggling reader needs to learn this strategy slowly, over time, and through many different examples.

So, why do readers summarize? Summarizing raises a reader's understanding beyond item level knowledge and moves it to a conceptual level. It is at the conceptual level that learning transfers and is best remembered (Erickson, 2002). The ongoing building and refining of summaries may help the reader develop generalizations (big ideas statements) of what was read, which in turn promotes deeper, more enduring understanding and the transfer of learning to new situations.

SAMPLE LESSONS FOR THE STRATEGY SUMMARIZING

Background: The following description of two fifth grade, small group reading lessons centers on the comprehension strategy summarizing. The teaching point in each lesson focuses on one or more of the skills embedded in summarizing. The goal is not only to teach summarizing, but to help students understand how this strategy can increase text comprehension.

The two lessons demonstrate the five steps of a small group reading comprehension lesson for struggling readers in practice. The teacher designed the lesson around previously identified student needs as evidenced in a Developmental Reading Assessment 4–8. Three students are in this fifth grade reading group. As lessons about summarizing continue for several more weeks, students will experience the skills that support summarizing in many different types of text. Finally, the reading level of the students in this group is approximately one year below a typical fifth grader.

Important note: These examples are not intended to be scripted instruction. The Gradual Release Lesson Procedure (Chapter 2) helps explicitly teach comprehension strategies; however, the effectiveness of the lesson hinges on a teacher's ability to make decisions based on his or her students' performance. Instruction needs to follow the child and be strategic. This is one of the many strategy lessons that might be used to teach the various skills of summarizing across different types of texts.

Example 3.1 Small Group Reading Lesson

Strategy: Summarizing.	Comprehension strategy emphasized during this lesson.
Focus Skill: Identifying important/essential information (main idea).	During previous assessments and observations, the teacher noticed that these students were having difficulty identifying important information or main ideas in text.
Instructional Activity: Discussion and oral retelling of important ideas.	Retelling is a good technique to use when introducing the skill identifying important information. It provides a *bridge* from students' social activities (talking) to written summaries.
Lesson Design:	The following five steps make up the lesson procedure and gradually release responsibility for reading work from the teacher to the students.
1. Explicit description of the strategy—when the strategy should be used: Teacher: *After reading many pages or a chapter of a favorite book or article, good readers often want to share what they have read with a friend. Remember when I have sometimes shared information with you about a book I am reading?* Students respond that they have. Teacher: *I didn't read the whole book to you, did I? Instead I gave you a summary. In summarizing, a good reader figures out the important ideas of the text, puts this information together, and, as briefly as possible, restates what was read in their own words—or paraphrases— as you have already learned to do.* *So, before a reader can create a good summary, he needs to know how to find those important events of the story. To do this, a good reader has to pause every once in a while, and notice the important ideas. Pointing out what is important will help a reader better understand and then share those essential ideas.*	Clear description of what the strategy and skill that will be taught in the lesson. The teacher gives a brief explanation of when the strategy is used and why it is important.
2. Teacher and/or student modeling of the strategy in action: Teacher: *Let me show you. I am going to read aloud the first paragraph from the Web site we visited in social studies earlier this week. Do you remember we were learning more*	The text selected for modeling is familiar text from a Web site they recently visited during a social

about Samuel Adams? I will show you how I figure out the important ideas I want to retell.

studies lesson. The teacher projects the text on the wall behind the reading table from her laptop. Note: Often the readability of content area material (especially textbooks) is too difficult for struggling readers, which is why the teacher chose an article from a social studies Web site covering the curriculum objectives. The article is at a lower readability level without compromising content. In choosing this article, the teacher is trying to support the students' social studies learning in addition to improving their reading skills.

I'll start by reading the first paragraph:
"Samuel Adams
Long before Thomas Jefferson drafted the Declaration of Independence in 1776, Samuel Adams wrote a school paper about the right for fairness and justice in government. Samuel developed his ideas about freedom while studying the theories of John Locke at Harvard College in the 1740s."

Teacher reads aloud the first paragraph.

Notice, teacher has control over the lesson at this point. Teacher is introducing this skill with single paragraphs.

Okay, let me stop and think about what the author is really trying to say here. I know this paragraph is about Samuel Adams, so he definitely is important. In the first sentence, the author wrote . . . "Long before Thomas Jefferson drafted the Declaration of Independence in 1776, Samuel Adams wrote a school paper about the right for fairness and justice in government."

The teacher begins to model the skill by thinking aloud as she rereads.

Teacher rereads first sentence aloud using computer cursor as a guide so students can follow along.

There are two famous names in this paragraph: "Thomas Jefferson" and "Samuel Adams." I know Thomas Jefferson is the author of the Declaration of Independence. . . .

Students nod.

Teacher: *So it seems the author is pointing out that Samuel Adams actually wrote about "the right for fairness and justice in government" long before the Declaration of Independence was written.*

Teacher models by thinking aloud how she finds important ideas.

When I reread the second sentence, "Samuel developed his ideas about freedom while studying the theories of John Locke at Harvard College in the 1740s," I see the author is

Teacher continues to model how she is determining the important information by thinking aloud.

(Continued)

Example 3.1 (Continued)

telling me where Samuel Adams learned about the ideas he put in his school paper. I think the author is telling me where Samuel Adams got the ideas for his school paper as a detail to make this article more interesting. Yes, I think the important information here is that Samuel Adams actually wrote about the right for fairness and justice in government long before the Declaration of Independence was written. *So, if I were going to tell Mr. Smith (the other fifth grade teacher) about this paragraph, I would first need to think about the important information I want to retell, and then paraphrase it, because I want to say it in my own words. I would say, "Mr. Smith, I learned Samuel Adams wrote about the right for fairness and justice in government long before Thomas Jefferson did!"*	Teacher explains her thinking about how to separate important information from supporting or nonessential information.
Teacher writes this statement down on chart paper. Teacher: *Gee! I had to do a lot of thinking about what I was reading to figure out the important information the author was writing about. I couldn't just pick out something I thought was interesting, like Samuel Adams went to school at Harvard College, because that was only a detail.*	
3. Collaborative use of the strategy in action: Teacher: *Okay, let's try figuring out the important information in the second paragraph together. Read this next paragraph together and think about the important information.*	Teacher is beginning to invite students to take more control over the lesson.
Students whisper read text orally in unison.	Teacher scrolls down so second paragraph is projected.
Students: *"After completing his studies, Samuel returned to Boston, Massachusetts, to work for his father. He began to question the fairness of the laws imposed by the governor, who was appointed by the British government. Samuel and his father spent several years trying to prevent British officials from taking their home and land."*	The teacher monitors students' oral reading and makes a notation about a student who appears to be having difficulty with some words.
Teacher: *What are you beginning to think is the important information in this paragraph?* Student 1: *I think it is important that Samuel began to question the fairness of the laws.*	

Teacher:	*Why do you think that second sentence is important?*	The teacher is closely guiding students as they attempt to identify important information on this short section of text. By raising questions and asking students to explain their responses, she is monitoring their understanding of the skill and strategy.
Student 1:	*Because he started to think they were unfair . . .* (stops)	
Teacher:	*The author said that . . .* (teacher uses cursor and reads aloud the second sentence of the paragraph). *Does everyone agree this is important or did the author include this information as a detail?*	
Student 2:	*I think* (reads aloud) *"Samuel and his father spent several years trying to prevent British officials from taking their home and land" is important.*	
Teacher:	*Why do you think that?*	
Student 2:	*Because losing his land and house would be important!*	
Teacher:	(turning back to Student 1) *Why didn't you select the idea of losing his land and house as being essential information?*	The teacher invites the first student into the discussion for a reaction.
Student 1:	*Because, ummm, because . . .*	
Teacher:	*Let's give him think-time.*	Teacher waits because the student is obviously cognitively engaged and trying to sort out his response.
Student 1:	*Because I think that is what he did after he thought the laws were unfair.*	
Teacher:	*Did everyone hear what J. said? He thinks that spending years trying to prevent the British officials from taking their home and land is a detail that supports the important idea that Samuel Adams began to question the fairness of the British governor.*	Teacher helps guide students' understanding of why the second sentence is essential information. Often the important ideas of a paragraph (especially in nonfiction) are in the first sentence. Students can become over-reliant on expecting that to always be the case, which is why this passage is a good sample.
Student 2:	*Oh yeah.*	

(Continued)

Example 3.1 (Continued)

Teacher: *Why didn't anyone say the first sentence, "After completing his studies, Samuel returned to Boston, Massachusetts, to work for his father," was an important idea?*	Teacher extends student's thinking by asking her to explain her reasoning. Having students explain their thinking helps clarify their understanding.
Student 3: *Because that is a detail that just tells us what he did after school.*	
Teacher: *Does everyone agree?*	
All three students show thumbs up.	
Teacher: *Exactly, this is not the really important information. If it were left out, we still would be able to understand that Samuel began to question the fairness of the British laws. Keeping track of the important information will help us remember this article and retell it later to our classmates.*	
Teacher adds sentence on chart paper.	Teacher makes a decision to continue in the collaborative step with the next paragraph as students are still tentative in identifying important information.
Teacher: *Let's work on the next paragraph together also.*	
4. Guided practice using the strategy with gradual release of responsibility:	
Teacher: *Now you read the next paragraph silently. We are going to rotate partners as we work through paragraph 4.*	After staying closely involved with students as they work to determine important information, the teacher now begins to step back and let students become more responsible for using the skill.
Teacher partners Students 1 and 2. She partners with Student 3.	
Once partners finish the paragraph, they quickly compare their discussions as a group and the teacher writes the paragraph's important information on the chart. We are going to work through paragraph 4 with a partner.	As the teacher rotates partnering with each reader, she continues to pull back support while carefully monitoring each student's application of the skill. Periodically she reinforces how identifying important information helps readers focus on the main ideas the author is addressing.

5. Independent use of the strategy:

Teacher: *We have learned that identifying important information helps us focus on the essential information the author wants to communicate, and it helps us summarize and retell the article, story, book, or movie to others. We will be practicing this skill with several different types of texts. Now I would like you to quietly read over the sentences on the chart that we decided represent the important information in this text. These six sentences are a lot shorter than the whole text, but they capture what was important, don't they? I want the three of you to hang the chart paper in the front corner of the room, and use it as you each take turns retelling this whole article in your own words. I will then be selecting one of you to retell this article with the class as a warm-up to our social studies lesson this afternoon. Although we all read it a couple of days ago, I want you to remind students about the important information.*

Because the students were familiar with orally sharing highlights of their favorite movies, weekend activities, and so on, the teacher decides to use retelling as an activity for independent practice. The teacher is confident that students will be able to retell the important information from their reading without her there. Subsequent lessons will give students many experiences in using the skill, identifying important information, across a variety of texts, and will integrate other skills that make up the strategy *summarizing*. When students gain more control over identifying important information, the amount of time spent on the first three steps of the lesson will slowly be shortened.

Teaching students to find important ideas in text is an ongoing process. Subsequent small group and whole class lessons will give students experience in finding important information in increasingly longer length texts, and in finding important ideas that are explicitly and implicitly stated.

As small group reading lessons in summarizing continued with this same group, the teacher determined the students were ready to move on to another summarizing skill: sequencing events. The lesson below reflects the first lesson introducing this new skill.

Example 3.2   Small Group Reading Lesson

Strategy: Summarizing.	Comprehension strategy emphasized during this lesson.
Focus Skill: Sequencing events.	Because the students had some whole class experience with sequencing narrative stories, she started this group's study of the skill with narrative text familiar to students.

(Continued)

Example 3.2 (Continued)

Instructional Activity: Graphic organizer and discussion.	A graphic organizer is a good technique to use when introducing the skill sequencing as it creates a visible record of the events, and gives students a framework for constructing their summaries. Caution: The events that are important to the story will be included in the graphic organizer, but a simple listing of events is not enough to make a good summary.
Lesson Design:	The following five steps make up the lesson procedure and gradually release responsibility for reading work from the teacher to the students.
1. Explicit description of the strategy — when the strategy should be used: Teacher: *We have been doing a lot of work with identifying important information to help us create a summary. Remember, in summarizing, a reader figures out the important ideas of the text, puts this information together, and, as briefly as possible, restates what was read in her own words.* *Another skill that helps readers summarize is sequencing events—or putting the important occurrences of the story in order. Remember when we learned about how important it is to sequence the steps of directions so we wouldn't make mistakes? Well, while reading we should also stop every once in a while to think about the sequence of events in a story.* *Sequencing events helps us see how the author is organizing the actions in the story. In other words, as you read a story and things happen, these are events.*	 Clear description of what the strategy and skill that will be taught in the lesson. The teacher gives a brief explanation of when the skill is used.

2. Teacher and/or student modeling of the strategy in action:

Teacher:	*Let me show you. I am going to use this graphic organizer to help me sequence the events in this fable. I'll start by reading the first paragraph of the fable* The Goose and the Golden Eggs. *(Teacher reads aloud.) Hmm . . . I see that the author is giving us a lot of information in this first paragraph: There are two people, a husband and wife, in this story; they are farmers; they are poor; they bought a goose; the next morning they went out and discovered a golden egg under the goose.*	The text selected for modeling is concise so the teacher can model the skill (sequencing events) across the entire text. The events are also easy to identify. Teacher models the strategy by thinking aloud as she reads the fable to the students.
Student 1:	*Man, why couldn't I get a goose like this?* (laughter)	Notice, teacher has control over the lesson at this point, but students do respond occasionally to the story.
Teacher:	*"Every morning they found a golden egg; they soon became very rich and had everything money could buy."*	
Student 3:	*I would buy new games, stuff for my room, lots of food, new clothes. . .* (laughter from other students).	
Teacher:	*Wow! The idea of having a goose that lays a golden egg every day sounds as exciting to me as it does to you! I am thinking that may be pretty important information in this first paragraph, but I need to think carefully about the events—what happened . . .*	
Students nod in agreement.		
Teacher:	*Because sequencing the events in this story will help me summarize the whole fable, I want to think more about this first paragraph. To do this, I need to leave out the extra information the author adds or repeats that makes the story interesting. Okay, here (Teacher points to lines in text.) the author gives me information about the characters so I can start getting a sense of who they are.*	Teacher begins to model by continuing to think aloud.
	The author tells me they are farmers, they are poor, and they are husband and wife. Because we already know that the main characters of a story lead the action, I am going to include the characters in the first event, but (Teacher points to lines in text.) the	Teacher continues to model the strategy by thinking aloud as she begins to construct the graphic organizer.

(Continued)

Example 3.2 (Continued)

author also tells me the wife goes into the farmyard each morning. This helps me to understand where the story is taking place, but I don't think it needs to included in the first event, because I already know that most people that would buy a goose live on a farm and that the characters are farmers. So I am thinking this is nonessential information. Right now, I am not including their trips to the farmyard as an event, but I may change my mind if this information becomes more important as the story continues. Right now, I only want to tease out the events of this paragraph and write it in the first box on my organizer in my own words. So, I am writing (Teacher models on white board.) *"A poor farmer and his wife bought a goose that laid golden eggs." Now I remember that signal words often give a clue of a new event, and I see the word "next" in this sentence.* (Teacher points to the sentence, "the next morning they went out and discovered a golden egg under the goose."). *There is also a shift here—some new action. They bought the goose but next they discovered it lays golden eggs and it kept doing it every day!*	Teacher explains her thinking. She also models how she needs to keep her thinking flexible as she continues to read.

Teacher thinks aloud how she is identifying each event as she writes it on the chart. |
| *Now I am ready to use this sequence of events to help me summarize this entire fable.* (Teacher points to each block in the organizer as she summarizes.) *This fable was about a poor farmer and his wife who bought a goose that laid golden eggs. Although the golden eggs made them very rich, the wife became greedy. They killed the goose thinking there was gold inside, but there wasn't, so that was the end of their gold!*

Does this summary put together the important events in this fable? | The teacher continues reading and modeling how she identifies each new event until she completes the four blocks of the graphic organizer. |
| Students all agree. | |
| Teacher: *Sequencing the events helped me put together my summary at the end, but did you hear how I added some of the important ideas when I mentioned each event? For example, did you hear how I added important information about the wife becoming greedy as a result of the event* (points to chart), *"the golden eggs made them very rich"? My summary is a lot shorter than the original fable; it is in my own words, and includes some important information.* | Teacher restates how sequencing events supported summarizing and how summarizing text helps good readers remember and understand what they read. |

Summarizing will help me remember this fable and think about what the important message is: That we should be thankful for what we have and not always want more!	
3. Collaborative use of the strategy in action:	
Teacher: *Okay, I want you to sequence the events in the next chapter of the book we were reading yesterday.* (Teacher hands out text and an organizer to each student.) *We will read this first page together and think about the events we want to include in the first box of our organizer.*	Teacher is beginning to invite students to take more control over the lesson.
Students quietly read orally in unison.	
Teacher: *What are you beginning to think is the first event on this page?*	The teacher closely monitors students' oral reading and other reading behaviors.
Student 1: *I think it is important that Molly tells Michael about Heather meeting Helen, and he thinks Molly dreamed it.*	
Teacher: *Why do you think that is the first event?*	The teacher is closely guiding students as they identify events from a short section of text. By raising questions and asking students to support their responses, she is monitoring their understanding of the skill and strategy.
Student 2: *Because that's what the characters start doing.*	
Teacher: *The author included a lot of other information in this section. How did you decide not to include it?*	
Student 3: *Because even though Molly was looking out the window, and it was foggy and she was barefoot, she was just standing there thinking . . .*	
Teacher: *That is quite significant. By including the other information, the author helps make us feel how spooky this whole thing is, but I agree, no action occurred until she decided to talk with Michael. Let's write this in our first box.*	
4. Guided practice using the strategy with gradual release of responsibility:	
Teacher: *Now you read the next page silently, and see if you can complete the next two boxes in our organizer.*	As the teacher individually checks in with readers, she continually draws

(Continued)

Example 3.2 (Continued)

Every once in a while, I will check in on each of you and ask you to explain how you identified the event you are sequencing.	each student back to the idea of how sequencing events helps a reader better understand the book (by making them think about how the author organized the story) and makes the text easier to remember.
Teacher periodically checks in with individual students as they read and complete their organizers.	The teacher stops the group for a brief moment to share an example of how one student revised what he wrote and his reasons for doing so. Students are taking responsibility for using the strategy on their own although the teacher is right there providing immediate and direct feedback.
5. Independent use of the strategy: Teacher: *We have learned that we can help create summaries by sequencing events in the story. Summarizing helps us better understand and remember what we read so we will be practicing this strategy on a lot of different types of books. Now I would like you to go back to your seats and read the last two pages of the chapter on your own. Complete the rest of your organizer as you read. Then I would like you to get back together as a group in the front corner, and share the information you included in your organizers. Compare yours to the others. Finally, in your writing journal, I'd like you to write a summary of this chapter using your story sequence organizer as a guide and include some important information. Tomorrow, in our reading group, I'll ask each of you to tell me how summarizing events helped you to better understand and remember this chapter. In your journal, you may also include any questions or comments you have about this strategy or skill for us to discuss tomorrow.*	The teacher is confident that students will be successful as they work independently based on the information she gathered during the reading lesson. Explicit instruction in the strategysummarizing will continue for several weeks using many different types of texts and skills with gradually longer sections of text. Each subsequent lesson will give students many experiences in using the strategy across a variety of contexts, and instruction in how to apply and integrate the other skills that make up the summarizing strategy. When students begin to gain more control over creating summaries and in understanding how summaries support comprehension, the amount of time spent on the first three steps of the lesson will slowly be shortened as the teacher releases more responsibility to the students. The multiple skills that support this strategy will be increasingly integrated, and small summaries will grow into summaries of entire texts.

SUMMARIZING ACROSS CONTENT AREAS

Middle school reading and content area teachers are always concerned about the struggling readers in their classes. If students have difficulty reading assigned text, it significantly affects their understanding of the discipline's concepts. In Chapter 1, the value of the Big Four as reading strategies that transfer and support content area reading is discussed. By leveraging these essential reading strategies, students will be able to be more successful with content area reading expectations.

The lesson below exemplifies how a middle school social studies teacher could help all students better understand content, but also provide support to students who have difficulty accessing the history textbook or following complex ideas. This lesson focuses on the summarizing skill "identifying important information and ideas" related to the American Revolution. This lesson also incorporates the Gradual Release Lesson Design and the use of a "conceptual lens." Erickson (2007) writes extensively about how teaching to conceptual "big ideas" that transfer across situations and through time facilitates deep understanding. Concepts serve as anchor points and organizers for the students who are overwhelmed by massive amounts of factual information. Once struggling readers grasp the critical concepts of a discipline, they have a system for bringing meaning to the chaotic stream of never ending facts. Students begin to see the relationships between the "big ideas" and the many different facts that exemplify them. Teaching to concepts along with in-class reading support, can make a world of difference in how successful these students are in their content area classes.

Example 3.3 Whole Group Eighth Grade Social Studies Lesson

Strategy: Summarizing.	
Focus Skills: Identifying and generalizing important information and ideas.	
Lesson Design:	The following five steps make up the lesson procedure and gradually release responsibility for reading work from the teacher to the students.
1. Explicit description of the strategy—when the strategy should be used: Teacher: *We have been reading and discussing the events of the American Revolution. We have learned many important facts about how our nation was formed. But facts of past events also provide "lessons of*	Teacher gives a clear description of what the class will be doing and connects the lesson's expectations to previous learning.

(Continued)

Example 3.3 (Continued)

history" that we can apply to our current lives. Today, we are going to use the "conceptual lens" of beliefs and values to help us summarize the important information from the American Revolution and find a "lesson of history."	
2. Teacher and/or student modeling of the strategy in action: Teacher: *Before we look at the American Revolution through the lens of "beliefs and values," let's practice using the conceptual lens of "migration." This is a concept that we studied previously. I am going to ask A., J., and C. to model their thinking for us. Can you come up to the front of the class?* *Okay, I'd like you three to talk with each other about what you have learned about the two questions on the board. "Why do people throughout the ages choose to "'migrate?'" and "Why did the colonists want to 'migrate' to America?" Make all your thinking public, so we really understand the rationale for your reasons. At the end, try to come up with an important idea you learned that still is important to people today. Everyone else, I'd like you to listen carefully to their discussion and be prepared to challenge if you hear something you disagree with. Go ahead . . .* Student 1: *Well, I am remembering that people migrate because they want a better life . . .* Student 2: *Yeah, and the colonists wanted religious freedom. They felt that would make their life better, because they weren't allowed to worship as they pleased. Some were getting persecuted.* Student 3: *People move for a lot of other reasons . . . money, jobs, freedom, to get away from people they don't like . . .* Class laughs. Student 1: *So the important idea we learned about migration is that people migrate to find a better life and to escape persecution.* Teacher: *Excellent! Class, how about a round of applause! By using the conceptual lens of "migration," you were*	Teacher is confident that the students she selects for modeling clearly understand how to scaffold their thinking to arrive at a "big idea." Students in this class listened to the teacher model thinking aloud numerous times in previous lessons.

able to think of many examples of history that not only applied to the colonists, but apply to why people migrate today and will continue to migrate.	
3. Collaborative use of the strategy in action:	
Teacher: *Now that you see how we can use a conceptual lens to find an important lesson or idea of history, let's think about the American Revolution through the conceptual lens of "beliefs and values." What is a belief? With your right elbow partner, please finish this sentence . . ." I believe . . ." Go ahead, you have 30 seconds to share.*	Although many students in the class may not need this step, it provides additional support to the students who become easily lost. It also provides additional reflection for those students who more readily grasp the new learning.
Stop . . . good job. I heard responses that included I believe I should be treated fairly; I believe in God; I believe in having choices; I believe you should treat people nicely . . . *Good job. I heard all kinds of different answers. . . . So, what is a belief?*	Teacher walks around monitoring student responses, especially those students she has concerns about.
Student 4: *It is an opinion.*	
Teacher: *And where do these strong opinions or beliefs come from?*	
Student 4: *From our experiences or from our parents?*	
Teacher: *Good thinking! Can I see a belief?*	
Silence for many seconds.	
Student 4: *Well, you will see me treating people nicely because I believe I should.*	
Teacher: *So, in how you behave, I might be able to see what you believe?*	Teacher gives plenty of time for students to process . . .
Several Students: *Yes.*	
Teacher: *And what would I see if you value something?*	The teacher's questions guide students' understanding about the concepts by asking them to get more specific.
Student 5: *You would see me fight you if you tried to take it away.*	

(Continued)

Example 3.3 (Continued)

Laughter.	Teacher now moves to applying the concept to text reading. Asking a student to begin by reading orally, gives the teacher the opportunity to stay closely involved and monitor students' understanding before transferring more responsibility to them.
Teacher: *Yes, so let's think about the conceptual lens "beliefs and values." Let's take a look at our next chapter about the colonists arriving in early America and look for evidence of strong beliefs and values. M., please read the first paragraph, and everyone listen for evidence of beliefs and values.*	
Student 6 reads.	
Teacher: *Did anyone hear an example of a strong belief or value?*	
Student 7: *It said that colonists left England because of religious persecution.*	
Teacher: *And what did we learn persecution means?*	
Student 7: *It means they were being punished because they did not want to belong to the Church of England—they wanted their own religion.*	
Teacher: *So what does this say about the colonists' beliefs and values?*	
Student 8: *It means they valued their religion so much they were willing to leave their country.*	
Teacher: *Who agrees? Thumbs up.*	
All students agree.	
Teacher: *We found an important idea about the colonists' beliefs and values. What about the beliefs and values of the English government? Did you find any evidence in the text about its position?*	
Student 9: *Well, they would rather have people leave their country than change the law.*	
4. Guided practice using the strategy with gradual release of responsibility:	
Teacher: *Exactly. So continue reading this chapter. I want you to use a post-it flag to mark where you find evidence of a strongly held value or belief. I will be walking around to see where you are using your post-it flags and ask you questions. Read to the end of page_____.*	Teacher quickly scans students to assess their progress, then devotes more time—one-on-one or in a small group in the back of the room—to the struggling readers in order to closely monitor their work.

5. Independent use of the strategy:	
Teacher: *Today, we used a new "conceptual lens" to help us identify important information or "lessons from history" that applied then, apply now, and will apply tomorrow. We started by remembering how you figured out the idea that* (writes on board) *"People migrate to find a better life and to escape persecution."* *Then we used the conceptual lens of "beliefs and values" to help us find more important ideas about the early colonists.*	The teacher recaps the essential elements of the day's lesson.
Now, get into your cooperative groups.	The teacher is still available to provide feedback to students as they develop a summary statement—a "big idea"—about the pages they read before they continue with the work as a homework assignment.
Points to directions on board.	
Teacher: *(1) I want each of you to share with your group all the post-it flags that gave evidence of the colonists' and the British government's values and beliefs. (2) When your group has finished sharing and discussing, go to your seats and finish this statement to summarize your discussion: "Strongly held beliefs and values _____." (3) Then for homework tonight, write a paragraph below your sentence stating other evidence from history (including today if you wish) that supports your summary statement.* *Questions . . . okay, let's get to work.*	The teacher provided the conceptual lens in this lesson, but as time goes on, students will begin to notice important text concepts on their own. This teacher shows how a meaningful comprehension lesson can be embedded into social studies text through a problem solving, thinking activity.

CONCLUSIONS AND REFLECTIONS

Summarizing is a complex strategy that requires the reader to reduce larger sections of text to the key concepts and essential information that are worth noting and remembering. It requires the reader to appropriately select and apply multiple skills. For example, questioning and synthesizing information are skills utilized throughout the process of creating a summary. Readers are constantly asking questions and connecting information such as: *What is the important information? What can I leave out? How does this fit/connect with what I just read? What will I remember about this information?*

Summarizing is an important comprehension strategy for readers of all levels. As students progress through grade levels, text becomes more complex, concept-dense, and demanding, so instruction in summarizing needs to be regularly revisited. By deliberately focusing instruction on the various skills required to create a summary across many different types of text, struggling readers will be on the road to better comprehension.

There is no one right way to create a good summary, but a summary has to mirror the thrust of the article and remain faithful to the author's emphasis and interpretation. When summarizing a reader is mentally keeping track of the important ideas being read and by doing so, comprehension and the retention of information are increased. Summarizing, also helps readers monitor their understanding of text as summaries of sections of text build on one another. This occurs while readers attempt to put together the various points the author is making (synthesize concepts and events) with what has gone before.

Readers' Questions and Author's Answers

Q: Is there one particular strategy I should teach first?

A: The strategies are not hierarchical so there is not an order to instruction. I have found, however, if students are not self-regulating their reading, it is a good place to begin comprehension instruction. Duke and Pearson (2002) tell us that even teaching one strategy well will benefit comprehension. This is due to the reciprocity among all the strategies and is also why there is not an order to teaching them. Through ongoing assessment and observation, you may notice students have more difficulty with a specific strategy. If this is the case, you may want to begin instruction addressing the weakness. Because these Four Powerful Strategies are so essential to all readers and to all types of texts, students will benefit from instruction in all strategies. The best thing to do is to get started!

Q: It is hard to find language that best explains the strategy and skill in the first step of the Gradual Release Lesson Procedure. If I write it out ahead of time, won't I sound stilted?

A: It is critically important to plan your explicit explanation of the strategy ahead of time because otherwise there is a tendency to ramble too long and/or muddy the explanation. The last thing we want to do to struggling readers is add to their confusion by not being concise and clear in describing what they need to do as readers. It is not unusual to see struggling readers fidgeting, yawning, or staring into space as a lesson begins. Reading has not been a pleasant experience for them so we need to be explicit in defining the strategy, why it is important, and when good readers use it. The Glossary is designed to help in planning the language you will use. Yes, your explanation may feel stilted at first, but things will begin to feel more natural as you become more confident and comfortable. As proficient readers, we no longer have to think about the processes we utilize as we read. As a result, it is easy to stumble when trying to explain a complex comprehension strategy off the cuff. Understanding what we go through as good readers and then putting this into words that will make sense to our students takes thought, time, and planning—but it is critical.

Next, Chapter 4 will explore another important comprehension strategy—*creating meaningful connections.* Although readers need to learn how to use all of the Four Powerful Strategies flexibly, efficiently, and in concert, instruction is initially designed to teach each strategy thoroughly and repeatedly while allowing for the spontaneous, natural integration of the other strategies and the skills embedded in them. Lesson examples in the next chapters will help to illustrate this further.

4

Putting the Strategies Into Practice

Creating Meaningful Connections

> *A novel requires you, the reader, to fill in an outline of words with vivid pictures drawn subconsciously from your own life, so that the story feels more personal. . . .*

—Barbara Kingsolver (1995)

Sometimes an author may craft such vivid and rich descriptions that images are almost constructed for the reader. When this occurs, readers may compare and contrast their own memories of images and connections with those painted by the writer. Other times an author leaves much to the imagination of the reader. In each situation, readers are actively engaged with text by using their schemata to compare, interpret, and comprehend what they are reading. Schemata are the mental representations of concepts, events, and experiences we hold in our memories (Rumelhart, 1980). Each new concept we learn, and experience we have, can be stored in our brain and serve as reference points to help us make the next situation more understandable. Capable readers activate and use their schemata by *creating meaningful connections.*

KEY TERMINOLOGY

Creating meaningful connections: The significance of the strategy *creating meaningful connections* lies within the transaction between reader and text—text language may suggest a connection that is entertainment for one person but may be unexpectedly emotional for another.

- **Imaging:** This skill is the process of forming sensory images (visual, tactile, auditory, etc.) while reading or listening.
- **Being aware of text language:** Authors use sensory language and other writer's craft techniques to help readers visualize ideas and make connections.
- **Activating prior knowledge/experience:** Schema is the background knowledge/information and experience readers activate and bring to the text.
  - **Previewing:** Previewing skills cause the reader to think about what he or she knows about the author, the topic, or the genre prior to approaching the reading task.
  - **Making text connections:** Keene and Zimmermann (1997) tell us readers comprehend better when they activate different kinds of connections (listed below).
    - **Text-to-Self (T-S):** Comparing and evaluating background experiences and images with information and descriptions presented
    - **Text-to-Text (T-T):** Comparing and analyzing characters, plots, themes, information, purposes, descriptions, writing styles, and/or versions of texts
    - **Text-to-World (T-W):** Comparing and considering text information with knowledge of the world
- **Questioning:** Questions that support the strategy creating meaningful connections include *How does this character's feelings compare to mine when I was in a similar situation?*
- **Synthesizing various types of connections and text:** This skill calls for putting together and making sense of information from texts and one's own connections with text to create new meaning.

WHAT IS CREATING MEANINGFUL CONNECTIONS?

The background knowledge and experiences one brings to the reading task play a role in each of the Four Powerful Strategies, and are very influential when a reader is *creating meaningful connections.* The noteworthy research of Rosenblatt (1978) and Iser (1978) helped us understand transactional theory, or the exchange of meaning that takes place between the reader and the text. The comprehension strategy creating meaningful connections exemplifies transactional theory.

As proficient readers read, they bring along their experiences and think about how the ideas presented in the text fit with what they know or believe. When creating meaningful connections, the reader may associate personal memories and feelings about people, things, or events in her own life with the author's words. The reader might also relate what is being read with text previously read or with her understanding of the world (Harvey & Goudvis, 2000; Keene & Zimmermann, 1997) The strategy creating meaningful connections triggers an individual reaction or response from the reader. Robert Probst (2004) reminds us that the reader's connections of personal experiences with text gives him a unique perspective and will greatly influence the shape (meaning) a text takes in his mind. This is not to diminish the role of the work itself. The author has the power to affect the reader's responses, guiding the reader in some directions and steering him away from others. "As we read, we find ourselves changing, revising impressions, accumulating information and insight and passing through a series of emotional states. . . . The flux and movement of reading [is] something the less sophisticated reader may have difficulty doing" (p. 22).

Just as it is important for teachers to take into consideration the background their students bring to text, it is important for students to understand that everyone's connections and images are unique and are affected by one's experiences. By sharing and discussing what the text reminds the reader of, the reader's understanding is deepened and other readers who are listening benefit from considering a new perspective or by gaining a new insight. *Creating meaningful connections* is a strategy that brings to light the reader's interactions with text and by doing so comprehension is strengthened and expanded in uniquely personal ways.

WHEN DOES A READER CREATE MEANINGFUL CONNECTIONS?

In addressing the question, when does a reader create meaningful connections, I am reminded of an experience I had in a book club I joined. We were definitely a mixed bag of readers. At our first gathering, one person in this newly formed group was quickly taken under the care of the others because (1) he was only trying this because his wife insisted, and (2) he was a self-proclaimed "nonreader." He hated reading all through school and openly admitted he rarely read as an adult unless it was something to do with work. I always find this an interesting phenomenon. How can a successful businessperson comfortably express a lack of interest in reading? Where did the schools fail this person? I recognize that my passion for literacy and helping struggling readers for much of my career may be one of the reasons why I respond so personally to comments like this, but it always makes me wonder how aliteracy (the ability to read but not choosing to do so) will affect creative minds.

At any rate, the book selection was about China (*Soul Mountain* by Gao Xingjian) and was a challenging text in terms of vocabulary and content. As book club members, we each kept a journal and periodically would get together to talk about our reading. On the evening of our first book discussion, the weather was bone chilling. As everyone arrived at the local Starbucks, we eagerly formed a tight circle around the fire and opened our notebooks, ready to share reflections. Listening to my friends talk about their reading and reviewing what I had written in my notebook, much of the sharing centered on the way we were all using the strategy *creating meaningful connections.* The meaningful associations readers often use to make connections are evident in three types skills that support this strategy: text-to-self connections, text-to-text connections, and text-to-world connections (Harvey & Goudvis, 2000), and they were all in play!

From each of the first three chapters, we shared quotes of some of the author's words, sentences, and phrases that we were personally struck by because of the especially rich, expressive language that needed to be lingered over, enjoyed, and appreciated. One "book buddy" commented how the author's word choice captured her senses and gave her an image to describe an emotion she could never put into words before. Some journal entries mentioned references to other books people remembered reading and now wanted to reread so they could compare information. One reader had jotted down questions in her journal that she wanted to research further in order to better understand the historical events presented in this book. One of my journal entries told of how the reading caused me to imagine how I might react if my government banned literature and censored all information (as was the case in the book). In my mind's eye, this thought sparked a connection to another book I had read about the Cultural Revolution in Iran in the 1980s (*Reading Lolita in Tehran: A Memoir in Books* by Azar Nafisi). Both texts helped me perceive how devastating losing choice would be. These examples from individual book club members reveal how personal creating meaningful connections are to a reader.

The group's nonstop chatter paused when we realized we were getting swept away by our enthusiasm and had yet to hear anything from our new book friend. We stopped to invite him into the conversation. What a shock we had! He opened his journal to show us the outline form he created for each chapter with the headings Theme, Setting, Voice, Characters, Summary, in large block letters. When he tentatively started speaking, his demeanor became formal and he read from his journal in a flat, unemotional voice. I suddenly had a flashback to how I felt presenting the dreaded book reports in high school (many years ago) where all discussion and questions were about *the book*, not about a reader's experience with the book. When a text is treated as a stable entity that contains all meaning, readers come to believe reading is one dimensional and is about reporting out "right" answers or retelling what was read. Typically, the struggling reader, or the reader who does not enjoy reading, places the control of comprehension within the text and believes the reader's job is to *tell the meaning* of the book rather than to personally live it.

Needless to say, our new book club member was not enjoying the book. We quickly decided we needed to abandon this text and find another selection to change his reading experience. We needed a selection where he could begin to feel what the strategy of creating meaningful connections is like. Our next selection, *River of Doubt* by Candice Millard, resulted in a very different response from our book friend. He not only jumped right into the conversation, but shared with us numerous adventures and mishaps he had as an avid rafter and hiker that helped him deeply understand what Roosevelt and his men were going through. He created connections with the anguish of the book's explorers as he related the story to some of his harrowing rafting experiences, and his connections were strengthened by bursts of plentiful images of the sense of fear, the sounds of cold, rushing water, coupled with the thrill of the challenge. This experience was a powerful reminder of how critical it is that kids are matched to the right books. But, in the discussion that followed, our new book friend regretted never before experiencing how richly rewarding reading a book can be. This revelation was the most heartbreaking, realizing that it took this long to have a positive experience with reading.

WHY DO READERS CREATE MEANINGFUL CONNECTIONS?

A good reader is not passive; rather, a reader who comprehends well reacts to what is being read in relationship to his or her own background experiences.

This process begins the moment a reader picks up a book. For example, when readers use the skill of previewing, they immediately begin thinking about what they already know about the topic, author, or genre. Previewing is where the strategy creating meaningful connections sets comprehension in motion.

When we affix a memory, a visual image, an imagined sound, smell, or emotion to text while reading, we are using skills that support the strategy creating meaningful connections and thereby deepen our interactions with text. Creating meaningful connections requires accommodations since the reader may continuously revise her views or connections as the text unfolds. When text is treated only as something to be interpreted, the relationships of the reader to the text, of the text to other texts, and of the text to life become lost or diminished. It is in these ranges of possibilities where creating meaningful connections gives a reader access to higher levels of understanding and stimulates the mental interchange of new thinking.

Creating meaningful connections is a catalyst for memory recall, for engaging a reader with text, and for making reading a deeply meaningful experience. Without this strategy, reading may feel like a chore that needs to be accomplished by trudging through each page unpacking what the author is trying to say. (As my book club friend seemed to feel.) The struggling reader needs to experience what it is like to create meaningful connections across many texts and needs to be taught how to use this strategy so that reading can be a more meaningful, pleasant, and interesting experience. Selecting books that we know students can relate to is important at the early stages of teaching this strategy. Additionally, a teacher may need to provide background knowledge if the student is unfamiliar with the major concepts in the text. Finally, it may take considerable modeling to show students how to use this strategy to deepen comprehension. Too often, in an attempt to please the teacher, students may become overly enthusiastic in their attempts at creating connections and get bogged down with minor details of the text.

SAMPLE LESSONS FOR THE STRATEGY CREATING MEANINGFUL CONNECTIONS

Background: The following is a description of a third grade, small group reading lesson. More time was spent in the first part of this lesson during the introduction of text-to-text connections, a new skill that supports the strategy of creating meaningful connections. As students progress with the new skill, the teacher will gradually release more responsibility to the students and consequently, the first two steps of the lesson will be brief, allowing more time for steps 3 and 4. There were five students participating in this reading group. All were reading approximately one year behind a typical third grader.

Important note: This lesson example is not intended to be scripted instruction. The Gradual Release Lesson Procedure (Chapter 2) is intended to show how lessons need to explicitly teach comprehension strategies. However, the effectiveness of the lesson hinges on the teacher's ability to make decisions based on how students respond. This is one of the many strategy lessons that might be used to teach the various skills involved in creating meaningful connections across different types of texts.

Example 4.1   Small Group Reading Lesson

Strategy: Creating Meaningful Connections.	Comprehension strategy emphasized during this lesson.
Focus Skills: Text connections: text-to-self, text-to-text.	Students have been working on text-to-self connections over the past five lessons. Text-to-text connections will be introduced in this lesson and linked to previous learning.
Instructional Activity: Coding the text.	Post-it notes will be used to code the text.
Lesson Design:	The following five steps make up the Gradual Release Lesson Procedure.
1. Explicit description of the strategy—when the strategy should be used:	
Teacher: *We've been talking about how good readers create meaningful connections while reading to help them understand the story. We've been focusing on text-to-self connections. Can anyone explain what happens when a good reader makes a text-to-self connection?*	Teacher asks students to recall the skill they have been learning that makes up this strategy.
Student 1: *When I made text-to-self connections, something in the book reminded me of something in my life that was kind of like what was in the book.*	
Teacher: *Yes. And all of you made lots of text-to-self connections in the books we have been reading. How did making a text-to-self connection help you as a reader?*	Teacher restates how the students were using skills that support creating meaningful connections.
Student 2: *Well, it made the book more interesting to me because it reminded me about stuff I know about, and it made me understand how characters feel. Some of the stories made me think of stuff I did and made me laugh thinking about it!*	The book the student is remembering is a wordless text that the teacher used to introduce students to the strategy creating meaningful connections. Sometimes wordless text or short, easy pieces are a good way to give students a clear sense of what the strategy is about. Subsequent lessons then slowly build in text complexity and length.
Teacher: *Which book in particular?*	
Student 2: *The* Carl and the Baby *book!* (laughs) *Because when my parents went out one night this babysitter and I jumped on my bed and did stuff I can't do with my mom. . . .*	
Teacher: *I remember you telling us about that when we read the* Good Dog, Carl *book.*	

Students nod in agreement and begin to tell other tales . . . remembering the books they have read. Teacher: *We can talk more about some of these other books later, but today we are going to learn about another kind of connection. Just as your personal experiences help you better relate to books, "text-to-text connections"* (Teacher writes words followed by "T-T" on white board.) *also help us make connections. Text-to-text connections are connections we make between the book we are reading and other books we have read. Sometimes when you make a text-to-text connection, it might be from a book you read on your own, or from a story that was read to you, or a movie that you saw.*	Explicit definition of text-to-text connection.
2. Teacher and/or student modeling of the strategy in action: Teacher: *Let me show you.* Teacher begins reading aloud *The Rough-Face Girl.* Student 1: (at page 3) *I am thinking this book sounds a lot like* Cinderella *because she had mean, wicked sisters too.* Student 3: *Yeah, I was thinking that in* Cinderella *there was a guy who everyone wanted to marry too.* Teacher: (Laughs) *I just was thinking about the book* Cinderella, *but I didn't even have a chance to say it! Okay, I am going to put a post-it note with T-T on it to remember the connection we made to Cinderella's mean step-sisters. As I read further, let's see how closely the two stories are connected.*	Teacher reads aloud. Teacher moves quickly into collaborative use of the strategy in action, as it is obvious to her that the students have some knowledge of the strategy.
3. Collaborative use of the strategy in action: Teacher: *As I continue to read, see what else you notice about this book and the book* Cinderella. *When you have something to share, raise your hand so we can talk about it and add a post-it note, okay?* Teacher resumes reading aloud. Student 2: *All these mean sisters think about is how pretty they are; that's the same with Cinderella's sisters.*	The teacher is beginning to invite students to take more control over their learning. In this first lesson, the teacher asks students what they *notice* about the two texts. This type of open-ended activity (asking students to raise questions) also serves as an assessment of how sophisticated students are with this skill. Open-ended responses like this provide opportunities for the teacher to closely monitor students' understanding.

(Continued)

Example 4.1 (Continued)

Teacher: (adds T-T post-it note to the page) *Does what you know about Cinderella help you picture what the Rough-Face Girl might look like if she could dress up like her sisters have?*	The teacher guides students' thinking about how text-to-text connections can deepen understanding.
Student 1: *I bet she would be pretty, with long dark hair . . . even if she has burns on her hands.*	
Teacher: *Does thinking about Cinderella help you understand this story?*	
Student 2: *Yes, because I know Cinderella had the same problems!*	
Teacher: *Right!* (Teacher continues reading and adds post-it notes when she models and thinks-aloud a connection to Cinderella. Students also add connections as the teacher reads.)	Teacher notes that Student 3 may be trying to force text-to-text connections with nonessential information. She will monitor this carefully.
Student 3: *Cinderella had special shoes made out of glass . . .*	
4. Guided practice using the strategy with gradual release of responsibility: Teacher stops reading aloud and asks the students to read the remaining five pages silently using the post-its to mark any T-T or T-S connections. **Teacher:** *Were all the parts of this story exactly like Cinderella?* **Students:** *No.* (They begin to discuss some of the differences when the teacher intervenes . . .) **Teacher:** *But there were things about* The Rough-Face Girl *that caused us to make connections to the story* Cinderella. *Let's go back and quickly look through our post-it notes.*	Teacher guides students in a brief discussion about the text-to-text connections they made on the post-its. The teacher focuses students' attention on how the images/connections helped them to better understand the story. Students are taking responsibility for using the strategy on their own although the teacher is right there providing immediate and direct feedback.
5. Independent use of the strategy: **Teacher:** *We have learned that we can make text-to-text connections about words, ideas, characters, and about what is important in a book.*	

(Continued)

Lesson Example 4.1 (Continued)

*Now, at the computer stations, I am going to have you watch with a partner the first 15 minutes of this DVD—*Prince Cinders. *After you and your partner have watched this, both of you talk about how it reminds you of the book* Cinderella. *The recorder* (Teacher appoints a recorder for each student pair.) *needs to make a list of some of the connections you talked about. Then you both need to talk about what you think the big, hairy monster is going to do next. Then, discuss which text-to-text connections you used to think about what the monster is going to do next. When you finish sharing, watch the last 10 minutes of the DVD and see how the ending compares to what you expected.*	The teacher is extending the lesson with another version of the Cinderella story. The humor of the animation film will not be fully captured if the students were unable to make text-to-text connections. The teacher will discuss the students' independent use of the strategy during tomorrow's small group reading lesson. Explicit instruction in text-to-text connections will continue across other genres until the teacher is confident the students understand how this strategy supports their comprehension.

Now, let's look at another small group lesson in a different grade level—Grade 5. This teacher has been working on the creating meaningful connections strategy for about a month. The students seem to have a solid understanding of the strategy and have had ample experience using the various supporting skills across a variety of types of text. This is one of the last lessons that will explicitly focus on creating meaningful connections. See how much more independent the students are earlier in the lesson and how the teacher is carefully noticing whether or not students are integrating the skills they have learned in previous lessons.

Example 4.2 Small Group Reading Lesson

Strategy: Creating Meaningful Connections.	Comprehension strategy emphasized during this lesson.
Focus Skills: The integration of the skills supporting the strategy that have been teaching points in lessons over the past month.	
Instructional Activity: Reflective journals and discussion.	Each student has a reflective reading journal that is used throughout the year.

(Continued)

Example 4.2 (Continued)

Lesson Design:	The following five steps make up the Gradual Release Lesson Procedure.
1. Explicit description of the strategy—when the strategy should be used:	
Teacher: *We have read a lot of different types of books over the past several weeks and focused our thinking on how we as readers are creating meaningful connections. Can anyone explain some of the skills we have been using to help us with this strategy?*	Teacher asks students to recall the skills they have been learning that are embedded in this strategy.
Student 1: *Text-to-text, text-to-self, text-to-world connections.*	
Teacher: *Who can expand on these skills—tell us what you did as a reader and how these skills helped you as a reader?*	
Student 2: *When I was thinking about some of the things in the books, like when we read that booklet about smoking, it made me think about a show I saw on TV with my mom where the lady died and her family tried to sue the cigarette company.*	
Teacher: *And what did that information connection you made with the world do for you as a reader?*	Teacher reinforces how the skill supported the strategy creating meaningful connections and how it benefited him as a reader.
Student 2: *Well, like I knew more about smoking from the TV show, so I was checking to see if it said the same stuff in the booklet.*	
Teacher: *That is a great example of how the skills from the strategy, creating meaningful connections, can help us read more critically.* *Does anyone else have one quick example of any of the skills we have been thinking about recently?*	
Student 4: *Well, I especially liked the* Knots on a Counting Rope *story because of all the words the grandfather used to tell the story of the night the boy was born . . . the storm and stuff like trying to find the midwife . . .*	

Teacher: *I know you especially enjoyed that story. Tell us more about those words and how they affected you as a reader.*	
Student 4: *They made me feel like I was right in the story because they gave me such details.*	
Students nod.	
Teacher: *Today we are going to read a book and I'd like you to think about all the skills we have used to help us with the strategy, creating meaningful connections. Let's look back at the chart we created of the different skills . . .*	Teacher points to the chart the group has created over the past month listing skills under the heading "Creating Meaningful Connections."
Teacher reads aloud the skills.	Ensuring students learn to strategically integrate all the strategies and skills is the long-range goal of teaching reading comprehension. As students begin to take control of their reading behaviors, they will naturally begin to integrate strategies and skills, but need the reinforcement and reminders in the transition to becoming independent readers.
Even though we focused specifically on one at a time to help us really think about what each one means, readers are using many of these skills almost simultaneously when reading. Remember how we started noticing how we were using more than one the more we read and thought about our connections? We said that is exactly what expert readers do and today, now that we have spent quite a bit of time on this strategy, I want you to use your reading journals to write down all the different skills you use as a reader when you create meaningful connections while you read. You only need to write the skill abbreviations and the page number in your reading journal. You can choose any one of the books on the table that you'd like to read today.	The teacher does not want to have students spending too much time away from text by writing sentences or lengthy reflections. Recording abbreviations and page numbers will keep interruptions from text to a minimum.
	The teacher has a pile of books within the students' reading range. Choice will give students more investment in their reading.
2. Teacher and/or student modeling of the strategy in action:	
Teacher: *Okay, now I'll model.*	
Teacher previews text.	

(Continued)

Example 4.2 (Continued)

Teacher:	*Wow! I am interested in this information for a couple of reasons: I have a niece who is a marine biologist and studies coral reefs, and I recently read another article about the danger coral reefs are in off the coast of Florida from the thousands of tires that were dumped in the water thinking they would act as reef and offer protection . . . but it isn't working. . . . I am going to be eager to see how what I learn in this article compares with what I know about my niece's work. . . . I'll write a "T-S" in my journal for that connection and also "T-T" for the connection with the other article I read. I'm also thinking about the title and looking at all the colors in this illustration. The author's language, "gardens of the sea," is making me picture the bottom of the ocean as a beautiful flower garden, like my neighbor's, that has many different colors and textures—I'll note that with a "T-L" for the text language and an "I" for imaging skills we talked about. Gosh! Do you see all the skills I've already used that helped me create meaningful connections?*	Teacher reads aloud title, author, and quickly scans the article. The teacher enthusiastically models her personal connections to the text, which is visibly contagious with the students.
	Does everyone get the idea? Here's the most important part: We talked a lot about the importance of the strategy creating meaningful connections in helping us better understand and remember what we read. The point is not to just make a long list of connecting skills. The skills I just used, text-to-self, text-to-text, imaging, and text language, helped prepare me to read so I can pay attention to new information and compare it to what I already know. I expect to learn something more about coral reefs from this article.	Teacher moves quickly into collaborative use of the strategy in action as it is obvious to her that the students are confident and understand the strategy.
3. Collaborative use of the strategy in action:		
Teacher:	*Now you select what you are going to read, get your reading journals, and open to the right page. . . .* *Everyone is set. Okay, I'll give you about five minutes to get started and then I'd like to have someone share their journal entry and talk about it. . . .* *How about J.? It looks like you have a couple of entries going after reading your first page. Will you tell us about them? Everyone, pause for a minute and listen in . . .*	Because the students know this strategy well, the teacher is turning the lesson over to them quickly. She still is checking in before letting them move into guided practice. She carefully observes students as they begin their reading.

Student 3: *I picked out this book about snowboarding cause I really want to learn more about it.*

Teacher: *And tell us about the skills you entered in your journal so far.*

Student 3: *Well, I put in T-L for text language because on this first page the words talk about how fast it is and what it feels like when you are snowboarding.*

Teacher: *Can you read a few of the words?*

Student 3: *Umm . . . you are slicing through the snow with the bitter wind and driving snow whipping at your face so that your cheeks feel little pin pricks . . .*

Teacher: *How does that language help you as a reader create meaningful connections?*

Student 3: *Well, the words made me know what it feels like to be going so fast and it makes me want to learn all the more.*

Teacher: *And what about the other notation you have from the first page?*

Student 3: *I put in a question mark for a question I was asking myself. I asked myself what kind of snowboard the kid in this book is using cause when I was at the store, I looked at different kinds.*

Teacher: *Right. And will you better remember this book because of the images you are getting from the book's language?*

Student 3: *Definitely! It sounds awesome!*

Teacher: *And how is the question you asked helping you as a reader?*

Student 3: *Well, it makes me want to read more and see if the snowboard is one of the kinds I saw.*

Teacher: *So you will be looking for specific information now as you read and compare it to what you already know. These are exactly the kinds of skills expert readers use when they are creating meaningful connections with the text they are reading!*

The teacher is repeatedly coaching the student to explain his thinking and reflecting. She also makes sure all the other students benefit from listening to this student's modeling.

Example 4.2 (Continued)

4. Guided practice using the strategy with gradual release of responsibility: Teacher: *Does everyone else understand? Okay, let's read on for the next 15 minutes and I'll periodically check in with you individually.*	The teacher quietly monitors the students and periodically checks in with each, one-on-one. While checking in, she periodically asks how the skills support connections to their reading and how they help them better understand what they are reading. Anecdotal notes are kept of these "on the run" assessment conversations. Anecdotal notes might include the skills each student is using (e.g., sometimes students focus too much on one skill, such as T-S, and making a note of this will remind the teacher to address this later), or the teacher might make a note about the text the student selected, and so on.
5. Independent use of the strategy: Teacher: *I listened to each of you explain how various skills helped you use the strategy, creating meaningful connections. Some of the other strategies we have talked about also came into your thinking. This was great work as very effective readers! You have really showed me how you learned to use these skills to better understand what you are reading.* *What I'd like you to do now, back at your seats, is to change roles. You are now going to be the author. I'd like you to start drafting a paragraph that you think would require a reader to use lots of the skills from this strategy.* *We have a lot of model texts in this pile that we've read over the last month. You can look through them to remind you of the characters and their experiences that were similar to yours. We also have some of the texts we read that reminded us of other books, movies because of the similar story structure, characters, and problems. Finally, you know your classmates as people, so you might write about a topic that you think most everyone in the class would connect with. After you write your paragraph, I'd like to look it over. Then you will exchange it with someone and have your partner explain how he or she creates meaningful connections to your piece. Do you have any questions? Good job everyone!*	The lesson extension puts students in the role of writer. They will now need to apply to their writing what they have learned about the skills that support the strategy creating meaningful connections. This activity will give the teacher further insight into the students' understanding of the skills and strategy. As they apply their learning to writing, their understanding will be deepened further. The teacher will review each student's paragraph so that any confusion or difficulties can be worked out prior to peer sharing.

CREATING MEANINGFUL CONNECTIONS ACROSS CONTENT AREAS

Many intermediate grade language arts teachers are beginning to reconsider *always* using the whole class, teacher-selected novel approach for good reasons. One-size-fits-all instruction does not respond to the needs, strengths, or interests of students [in Grades 3–6] (Ivey & Fisher, 2007, p. 2). For decades, language arts classrooms have been wedded to the practice of requiring students to critically analyze a core list of teacher-selected literature. Instruction in this model focuses more on the book than on the individual reader and writer.

There are many ways we can begin to use small group lessons within upper grade language arts classrooms. Restructuring intermediate grade language arts classrooms so that there is time for the teacher to provide explicit instruction with small groups of students is essential if we are ever going to break the cycle of failure for struggling readers. The next lesson is an example of how this might be accomplished.

The lesson below comes from a sixth grade language arts class. This class started with whole group instruction in metaphors with a Gradual Release Lesson Design. When they broke into small groups for guided practice, the teacher separated out the students she knew needed closer monitoring. The Gradual Release Lesson Design allows the teacher to make sure students are capable of and responsible for doing the reading work. The fifth step, independent practice, is carefully planned in order to reinforce the students' role in learning to be independent readers.

Through teacher modeling and repeated practice with a variety of texts (first with texts that show obvious examples of the strategy and skill being taught—later in texts with less overt examples), the progress of struggling readers can be accelerated.

Example 4.3   Whole Group Mini Lesson—Sixth Grade Language Arts

Strategy: Creating Meaningful Connections.	Comprehension strategy emphasized during this lesson.
Focus Skill: Being aware of text language (metaphors).	
Instructional Activity: Modified readers workshop.	
Lesson Design:	The following five steps make up the Gradual Release Lesson Procedure in this mini lesson.

(Continued)

Example 4.3   Whole Group Mini Lesson—Sixth Grade Language Arts

1. Explicit description of the strategy—when the strategy should be used:	
Teacher: *We have only been in our poetry unit for a few days, and we've already found image-laden poems that give us a real appreciation for how an author's use of language can support how we create meaningful connections to what we read.* *Today, I have five different poems or lyrics from songs that will be familiar to you. These examples are up here on the front table. We will be using these in your groups today, but first I want to talk about what you will be doing in your groups.* *All eyes up here . . .*	Teacher introduces the focus skill of the mini lesson and explains how the skill supports the strategy creating meaningful connections.
Today we are going to focus on a specific language technique, metaphors, that writers use to communicate deeper levels of meaning. We defined metaphor a couple of days ago. . . . Can someone read our definition from the board?	Teacher is giving explicit instructions about what the students will be doing in this lesson. This makes the expectations for the students clear, up front.
Student 1: *An indirect comparison between two or more seemingly unrelated subjects that creates a powerful picture for readers.*	
Teacher: *Thanks . . . and we looked at a few examples. Well, today we are going to think further about what metaphors do for us as readers. As you read your poems in your groups you are going to discuss how you relate to the writer's use of metaphor and how the language helped you better understand and make connections with the poem.*	
2. Teacher and/or student modeling of the strategy in action:	
Teacher: *I'll read a short poem and model my thinking as I pay close attention to the text language, especially the metaphors, and how they help me create meaningful connections to this poem.*	The teacher gives students a clear purpose for listening.

Teacher reads aloud poem, "Creativity" by StarFields. "On the wall, etc." *I see how the author is comparing a shadow on a wall to a pen writing a story . . . Through this metaphor I see how the branch that casts the shadow on the wall must be swaying in the wind because the shadow is moving, dancing. . . . and the person watching this shadow is imagining a pen moving and dancing across a page; the ink of the pen is the light that comes and goes as the shadow moves. . . . By paying close attention to this language I can see not only what the author is saying, but it is making me remember as a child lying in my bed, early in the morning before anyone else was awake, and watching shadows come and go on my bedroom wall. I used to imagine all kinds of creatures and trees and faces emerging. This author's language brought that all back to me. Those memories are hard to put into words, but the author captured my feelings and images in this poem, which is why I appreciate what it says in its simplicity.*	By listening to the teacher thinking aloud, students are able to hear how she is interpreting and how it helps her create meaning by creating meaningful connections with the poem. .
3. Collaborative use of the strategy in action: Student 1: *I used to do the same thing in my bedroom . . .* Teacher: *Isn't that a great thing—when a writer can express what so many of us feel and then by reading, all those memories come back?* *Let's look at another short poem together. This time I will ask for your help in explaining the metaphor. . . . Let's read this aloud in unison.* Teacher and students read aloud "Pitcher," by Robert Francis. Everyone: *"His art is eccentricity . . ."* Student 2: *What is eccentricity?*	Because the students know this strategy well, the teacher is turning the lesson over to them quickly. She still is checking in before letting them move into guided practice. She carefully observes students as they begin their reading. The teacher brings students into the interpretation of the next poem and through scaffolding questions, helps a student who needs some assistance in understanding the metaphor.

(Continued)

Example 4.3 (Continued)

Teacher: *Who can help? Have you ever heard of someone being eccentric?*	
Student 3: *Yeah, like weird or way out there . . .*	
Teacher: *Can you give me an example?*	
Student 3: *Well, in art class we talked about an artist, you know you guys, what's his name? And anyway, Mrs. S. said he was considered eccentric because he painted in a way no one ever saw before . . . splashing big blobs of paint all over.*	
Teacher: *So, K., do you think you can explain what eccentricity means now?*	
Student 1: *His art is weirdness?*	
Students laugh.	
Teacher: *Okay, let's go with that . . . weird or strange. What is the writer comparing in this poem? Is he really talking about a baseball pitcher?*	The teacher continues to ask students to think aloud and lets them know they are doing a good job in trying to make sense of the language.
Student 1: *No, because a baseball pitcher wouldn't want to not hit the mark he is aiming at.*	
Teacher: *Good thinking. There clearly is a contradiction between the title and the "he" in the poem. So, go back to our definition and think what other words give us clues about what might be being compared to a pitcher—since we know a pitcher would definitely want to hit his mark—the pronouns in the poem must be referring to something else. Tell me what you are noticing by focusing on the language the author is using in the first two lines.*	The teacher is scaffolding students' thinking by narrowing their attention to specific words and sentences.
Teacher reads aloud.	
Teacher: *How not to hit the mark he seems to aim at.*	
Student 1: *Well, it's like saying it's strange that he doesn't want to hit the mark everyone thinks he is aiming at.*	
Teacher: *Why do you think that? Can you explain?*	
Student 1: *Well, it says right there, his aim is "how not" to hit the mark he seems to be aiming at . . .*	

Teacher: *What is another way of saying that in your own words?*	
There is a long pause.	
Student 4: *It's like his goal is not to do what he's supposed to be doing, but he is looking like he's trying?*	
Teacher: *How many of you agree that is a possibility?*	
Other students nod in agreement.	
Teacher: *That's a good thought; let's keep that in mind as we keep going . . .*	
Teacher continues discussion through the next two lines.	
Teacher: *Okay, we discovered some words that don't fit with the behaviors of a pitcher, right? Let's circle those phrases that seem strange. . . . What would you suggest I circle?*	Now that the gist of the poem is beginning to emerge, the teacher goes back to make patterns more obvious to students by having them identify phrases for her to circle and then having them think about what the phrases have in common.
Student 5: *Not to hit the mark.*	
Teacher: *Excellent. We know this is not the behavior of a good pitcher. What about the next line?*	
Student 2: *Avoid the obvious.*	
Teacher: *Absolutely!*	
Teacher and students continue in this manner with the poem.	
Teacher: *Now let's look across the phrases we circled. What do you think these words might be describing?*	
Student 4: *Me, when I don't want to clean my room!*	
Students laugh.	
Teacher: *Yes! I think you are creating a connection! Why do you do things like this when you don't want to clean your room?*	
Student 4: *I'm stalling.*	

(Continued)

Example 4.3 (Continued)

Teacher: *Could the writer's metaphor be about dragging your feet or putting off the things you are trying to avoid? Let's read it through quickly all together and see if this makes sense.* Class reads poem aloud in unison. Teacher: *Can we see how the writer might be comparing a pitcher, who is precise, knows his mark, and consistently aims for it, to someone who is doing the opposite . . . like someone who does everything to avoid getting homework in on time and keeps changing techniques for not getting it done?* Students laugh. Teacher: *You did a great job. This is how writers can use metaphors to help readers make connections and find deeper meaning. It takes some thinking, but it makes writing so much more interesting. Could someone else have a different interpretation? Yes, absolutely, because we all bring different experiences with us to the poem . . .*	The teacher restates the student's connection to the poem and expands on it with another example. Finally, the teacher closes by reiterating how metaphors can cause readers to create meaningful connections to text, which result in a deeper understanding. She also points out that different readers may have different interpretations due to the varying backgrounds they bring to their reading.
4. Guided practice using the strategy with gradual release of responsibility: Teacher: *This first part took longer than I thought, so I'd like you to get into the groups I assigned you to and get right to work. I will give each group a poem and then let's get going. I'll be around checking in on each group's progress.*	The teacher has carefully grouped students so four groups are heterogeneous. One group is homogenous and is made up of three students she knows will need extra support in understanding metaphors. After a couple of lessons, she will reassign all student groups and integrate these students back into heterogeneous groups. The poems she distributes are within all students' reading level. The teacher moves from group to group listening in and coaching as necessary, but spends most of her time with the small group of struggling readers.

5. Independent use of the strategy:	
Teacher: *How interesting it was for me to listen in on your small groups today! I am so impressed with your thinking and with the way you are really digging into the poems' metaphors and making your own connections. Some of you also talked about the images the metaphors created in your mind. Metaphors make us stop and think. They are a way that poets grab us as readers and help us comprehend the emotions and feelings that are sometimes hard to express in words. Tonight as homework, I want you to think through the discussions you had in your groups. Write down some of the things you talked about so you don't forget. Tomorrow I will give you a short time back in your small groups to compare your notes and plan how you will share your discussion with the whole class. Each group will have five to seven minutes to present, and that includes reading your poem before you start sharing your discussion. This means you will only have time to share the highlights of your discussion. Remember, you need to also talk about how the metaphor helped you as a reader in creating meaningful connections. Nice job class!*	The teacher is guiding student thinking to a higher level by having them practice what they learned in an activity that will further develop their understanding.

CONCLUSIONS AND REFLECTIONS

I often think back on the book club experience I described earlier in this chapter. I worry that too many students still go through school learning to decode words and to find the surface meaning of text, but never fully experience the joys and personal fulfillment that comes when reading is not a laborious task and when they have experiences with books that genuinely capture their interests. When comprehension is difficult or not well understood, the motivation to read and complete assignments shuts down (Robb, 2000). If students can read, but they perceive themselves to be weak readers or if they have not felt reading as a satisfying experience, aliteracy is often the result. And, aliteracy is a growing problem in the United States (Moser & Morrison, 1998). This comes at a time when our country needs workers who can read large quantities of information quickly, think critically about that information, and synthesize the concepts to spark innovative and creative ideas, so we can remain a viable participant in the twenty-first century knowledge society. There is a significant amount of evidence that shows that when comprehension instruction is effective, students do increase their capacities to understand and experience reading success.

The strategy *creating meaningful connections* can be an engaging way to begin explicit comprehension instruction. Initially introducing instruction in this strategy in an open-ended manner allows you to observe and discuss with students the types of connections they are creating with various texts. Also at the onset of the year, developing relationships with students to learn about their interests and background experiences helps you select texts that support their ability to create meaningful connections. In the early stages of learning this strategy, it is especially important to match readers to books that will help them be easily aware of the skills they are using. If the text is beyond the scope of students' backgrounds and interests, it is critical to give them the prior knowledge they need so that they can create connections to their reading.

As instruction continues, students learn to use the creating meaningful connections strategy before, during, and after reading to maintain a high level of engagement with the text and for reflection. Students soon begin to realize how creating meaningful connections can make reading more interesting, emotional, memorable, and understandable. When students begin to argue against an image that an author depicts or can cite specific examples of the connections they are making—from their life experiences, other texts, or their knowledge of the world—that contradict or support what they are reading, you know they are creating meaningful connections.

Readers' Questions and Author's Answers

Q: What is the best way to assess my students' progress?

A: Daily observation in a small group setting is one of the best ways to monitor students' progress. Gradually releasing responsibility of the lesson's teaching point allows a teacher to closely watch students as they put their learning into practice.

Struggling readers are more apt to go unnoticed in whole group instruction. In front of a class of peers, many of the students who struggle with reading beyond third grade have learned to "look like a capable reader" by burying their heads in their books hoping they will not be called on. Others have learned how to distract attention from their reading problems by acting out or by being the class clown. Instruction in small groups or one-on-one helps prevent these students from slipping through the cracks and allows more student interaction and teacher support.

Benchmark assessments that are beneficial include the Qualitative Reading Inventory (QRI), the Developmental Reading Assessment 4–8, and teacher made tasks that assess comprehension. Authentic activities that ask students to write about their reading or to give an oral presentation are also valuable assessment tools. By linking reading and writing and oral expression, students' understanding is further strengthened and teachers gain valuable information about the progress students are making.

Too often reading comprehension is assessed but not explicitly taught. Explicitly teaching comprehension is a first step; assessments should then match the teaching points of the lesson.

Q: How do I select the appropriate text for students?

A: Text needs to be selected that students are able to read with at least 90 percent accuracy. If the text is too difficult, the students will exhaust themselves as they labor to decode challenging words and unfamiliar vocabulary. They will have no energy left to think about how they are reading strategically. Text needs to appeal to the interests of the reader and initially should exemplify the teaching point of the lesson. For example, you wouldn't want to use a text with highly familiar content that students already comprehend to teach the strategy self-regulating because students will have no need to problem solve or fix up anything. On the other hand, this same selection might be perfect for teaching the strategy creating meaningful connections.

Chapter 5 now examines a closely linked strategy—*self-regulating.* Many students in Grades 3–8 may have had several years of instruction in self-regulating as it is an essential early reading strategy. Self-regulating never loses its importance, however. As reading materials in the upper grade levels become more complex and dense, and as text information becomes increasingly unfamiliar to students, teachers need to be sure students have not forgotten reading needs to always make sense. The strategy self-regulating is about ensuring reading always makes sense and how to fix comprehension if it does break down.

5

Putting the Strategies Into Practice

Self-Regulating

Readers of all ages need to be conscious of when they are not creating meaning. The ability to self-monitor meaning enables students to select and use strategies to improve comprehension.

—Maryann Manning (2002)

The strategy *self-regulating* is operationalized in all reading. You have been using this strategy of self-regulating while reading this book, but you are most likely not even consciously aware of the skills you are using to keep track of meaning. This is because comprehension strategies and skills typically go "underground" for proficient readers. Self-regulating skills become imperceptible unless you need them.

KEY TERMINOLOGY

Self-Regulating: This strategy requires an active awareness and knowledge of one's mental processes (metacognition) and knowing what to do in order to accomplish the goal of comprehension.

(Continued)

(Continued)

- **Knowing self as a learner, the reading task, and reading strategies:** If there is a conscious awareness of what we know about ourselves as a learner, we are on our way to learning how to self-regulate. Knowing our strengths and weaknesses allows a proactive plan to be developed that will support success.
- **Knowing the purpose for reading:** The skill of knowing the purpose for reading directs which monitoring skills need to be used and the reading rate.
- **Looking back, rereading, and reading ahead:** Most struggling readers believe that something must be wrong with them if they must read a textbook chapter or article more than once or look back over text features they previously skimmed. Good readers, especially when reading less familiar topics, recognize that reading material once is not enough.
- **Predicting, confirming, clarifying, and revising:** Making predictions means describing what one thinks will be revealed next in the selection based on clues from the title, illustrations, and text details.
- **Problem solving words, phrases, or paragraphs:** Problem solving skills may take many forms. Using the meaning of prefixes, suffixes, and word roots may help unlock an unknown word. Proficient readers also use information from text (context) to decipher unfamiliar words.
- **Cross-checking multiple sources of information:** This self-regulating skill requires bringing together at lease three sources of text information simultaneously.
- **Adjusting reading rate:** The skill of knowing when and how to skim and scan for specific information and when to read more slowly is closely tied to the purpose for reading.
- **Questioning:** Questions that support the self-regulation strategy include: *What is going on in the text? Why I am reading this text? Are there ideas that don't fit together? Are there any words I don't understand? Is there information that doesn't agree with what I know?*
- **Synthesizing text with background information:** Meaning is being constructed and adjusted constantly as a reader analyzes text information against the background information he or she brings to the text.

WHAT IS SELF-REGULATING?

Metacognition refers to higher-order thinking, which involves active control over one's cognitive processes. Self-regulating is a metacognitive activity. When readers are self-regulating, they have the ability to scrutinize, regulate, and direct themselves to a desired goal before, during, and after reading. A student demonstrates self-regulation (metacognition) by articulating the strategies and skills used to read and understand text and by fixing problems that interfere with comprehension.

John Flavell's work with metacognition (Livingston, 1997) helps describe the complexity of the strategy *self-regulating.* Use of this strategy begins at the *knowledge level:*

1. How well you know yourself as a learner. For example, you know that as a reader, you need a quiet, distraction-free setting.

2. How well you recognize the demands of the reading task. For example, you are aware that you will need a dictionary close at hand while reading a scientific article on a topic about which you know very little.

3. How well you recognize the strategies necessary to accomplish a learning goal. For example, you consciously think about the strategies you will need to read challenging text. This knowledge helps a reader approach an unfamiliar reading task with a plan in mind.

At the *application level,* self-regulating involves making sense of one's reading. The strategy self-regulating encompasses the skills and processes a reader uses to regulate—from preparing for a reading task to evaluating personal progress toward understanding. At the most basic level, a reader needs to be aware of remaining mentally engaged with the text. It doesn't take independent readers long to realize when their thoughts have drifted away from the task of reading. At this point, the good reader will snap back and regroup to find the point of departure. Struggling readers often continue to go through the physical motions—eyes sweeping across words and hands turning pages—only to get to the end before realizing their minds were somewhere else, and they have no recollection of what was read.

Once readers recognize where reading has broken down, the next step is to work out the problem. There are a number of fix-up skills that support the self-regulating strategy. Often a reader employs more than one, but the point is that a proficient reader will do what it takes to make sense of text. Self-regulating is a significant component of comprehension.

WHEN DOES A READER SELF-REGULATE?

When the reader tries to use different strategies and skills to make sense of text, he is self-regulating. A lot has been learned about the strategy self-regulating by listening to good readers read orally and then talking with them (having them think aloud) about their errors, their ability to make self-corrections, and all that went on in their head as they worked to create meaning.

In the mid-1960s, Ken Goodman (1986) introduced the term "miscue" after he found that many mistakes are not random. Often patterns emerge when studying a reader's inaccuracies that provide insights into what the reader is attempting to do (or not do) to make sense of text. Miscue analysis became a way of closely observing, recording, and analyzing early oral reading behaviors to assess how readers use specific cues such as syntax, semantic information, and graphophonics to create meaning. The oral reading errors a student makes can represent which reading skills are more highly developed than others. Miscues can be analyzed to suggest which strategies the reader is using or lacking, and what kinds of additional instruction might be helpful. This is a great informal assessment technique that can provide insights into a reader's ability to self-regulate.

Raising awareness that the reading needs to be constantly monitored is a first step for effective self-regulating. Although it may not be apparent until meaning breaks down, an independent or advanced reader is always cognizant of making meaning of text. At the point where meaning is lost, self-regulating fix-up skills are used to get the reader back on track. Fountas and Pinnell (2001) point out that the strategy self-regulating becomes increasingly complex as readers become more proficient:

It [self-regulating] might entail drawing on literary knowledge to determine whether a plot is probable or a character believable. It might mean matching the text information with what is already known about that period of history in which the text is set to determine the authenticity of the piece and understand it more fully. Readers might surmise whether a text reflects a particular author's style or revel in the clever way an author has mixed two genres. . . . Monitoring understanding centers on an active engagement with the author of the text while continuously asking, "How does my understanding fit with what I am reading?" (p. 311)

We can learn much about students from noticing what they do when they encounter difficult words and longer-length, unfamiliar text. The bottom line is that self-regulating occurs when readers actively pay attention to their own reading and make sure comprehension is intact.

WHY DO READERS SELF-REGULATE?

Self-regulating helps readers check and control their comprehension on an ongoing basis and adjust their reading strategies to maximize comprehension. This is why students need to know that all readers run into difficulties while reading. Confusion is a natural part of reading. Good readers are more accepting of ambiguity or gray areas of text, especially at the beginning when a reader doesn't yet have a good foothold on the story line. Good readers are also more persistent in problem solving. Struggling readers, on the other hand, often feel they are the only ones who have trouble and are quickly overwhelmed. If we can break the cycle of helplessness for struggling readers, they will be on the road to better comprehension.

Because the strategy self-regulating plays a critical role in all successful learning, it is important that it be explicitly taught to students who do not demonstrate metacognitive control. Self-regulating is essential to understanding how reading works and to becoming a strategic reader who comprehends well.

SAMPLE LESSONS FOR THE STRATEGY SELF-REGULATING

Background: The following description of two third grade, small group reading lessons centers on the comprehension strategy self-regulating. The teaching point in each lesson focuses on one or more of the skills embedded in self-regulating. The goal is not to only teach the strategy, but to help students understand why self-regulating is essential to text comprehension. To achieve this learning, students need to practice the many different skills embedded in self-regulating. By practicing these skills across many different types of text, the transferability of self-regulating is reinforced.

The next lesson demonstrates the five steps of a small group reading comprehension lesson for struggling readers. The teacher designed the lesson around previously identified student needs as evidenced in a Developmental Reading Assessment 4–8 and classroom observations. Five students are in this third grade reading group. As lessons about self-regulating continue for several more weeks, students will experience the skills that support self-regulating across many different types of text. This is one of the many strategy lessons that might be used to teach the various skills of self-regulating. Finally, the reading level of the students in this group is approximately one and a half years below a typical third grader in the class.

Important note: These examples are not intended to be scripted instruction. The Gradual Release Lesson Procedure (Chapter 2) helps explicitly teach comprehension strategies; however, the effectiveness of the lesson hinges on a teacher's ability to make decisions based on his or her students' responses. Instruction needs to follow the child but it also must be strategic. This is one of the many strategy lessons that might be used to teach the various skills of self-regulating across different types of texts.

Example 5.1 Small Group Reading Lesson

Strategy: Self-Regulating.	Comprehension strategy emphasized during this lesson.
Focus Skill: Questioning.	Through the Developmental Reading Assessment, Second Edition (DRA2) running record assessment and previous classroom lesson observations, the teacher realized students are not consistently asking themselves questions to support *self-regulating*.
Instructional Activity: Discussion and think-aloud.	By beginning with discussion and practice making thinking public, all students will hear questions they should be formulating in order to self-regulate.
Lesson Design:	The following five steps make up the lesson procedure and gradually release responsibility for reading work from the teacher to the students.
1. Explicit description of the strategy—when the strategy should be used: Teacher: *Today we are going to look more closely at the strategy self-regulating. Self-regulating teaches us to check our understanding of what we are reading and to fix our reading when things don't make sense. This is an important strategy that all good readers use because reading always needs to make sense. One skill that helps us self-regulate is questioning.* *Excellent readers think of questions before, during, and after reading, because the right questions can help readers check up on their understanding and fix tricky things that don't make sense.*	Clear description of the strategy and skill that will be taught in the lesson. The teacher gives a brief explanation of when the strategy is used and why it is important.

Example 5.1 (Continued)

2. Teacher and/or student modeling of the strategy in action:	
Teacher: *Let me show you. I am going to read aloud this short poem. I will think out loud the questions I ask myself as I try to understand the poem and any tricky parts that aren't making sense. You listen carefully while I do this, okay? All eyes and ears on me.*	The teacher holds up the text so everyone can see. By introducing questioning with a short piece of text, it allows the teacher to model questions that can be used before, during, and after reading. Although that might be more than is needed for some students, for this third grade group it is appropriate.
Students nod in agreement.	
Teacher: *Before I start reading, I am asking myself questions that will help me gather information and get a focus before I read. I am asking myself the question, "What could this poem be about?"*	Notice, teacher has control over the lesson at this point. Teacher is introducing this skill with a short poem that students in the group will relate to and understand. By starting with a simple, readable text, students will clearly understand what the teacher is modeling.
I see a huge birthday cake with a very big, happy man looking at it. I am also asking myself, "Why are there little clouds coming from the boy's and cat's heads at the bottom of the page and go up to the picture of the big man in front of the cake?" I am wondering, "What do I know about pictures like this?"	
Well, I remember seeing bubbles used in a story once and it was to show the character's thoughts. I am thinking the picture of the big, happy man with the huge cake might be something the boy is thinking or dreaming about, but I need to read more to find out.	
Here's the title. A G-i—, hmm, I am not sure of this word. I am asking myself the question, "Do I see any word parts I know?" I see the word "ant"—I'll try it again using what I know. G-i-ants. This still doesn't make sense to me. I am asking another question, "What else can I do as a good reader?"	The word the teacher is problem solving is the "Giant's." The teacher mispronounces the word "Giant" with a hard G and long i sound.
I am looking at the picture to see if it helps me. I see that big man with that huge cake. I am asking myself, "Could he be a giant?" Let me go back and try that and see if it makes sense.	Teacher is modeling how using known word chunks combined with information in the picture helps solve a tricky word.
(Teacher reads title): "A Giant's Cake" *Yes! That makes sense. I'll keep reading . . .*	Teacher models rereading title to clarify and check understanding.
Teacher continues to read.	
Teacher: *And m-u-m—that's a funny word . . . gives a party . . .*	

I am asking myself the question, "Could this be the same as mom?" It sounds a little like that and it would make sense because moms often give kids parties. I think it must be another way of saying mom—like mommy or ma. . . . And mum gives a party. I'll keep reading now . . .	Teacher explains her thinking about integrating background information and association to make sense of a tricky word. Teacher continues in this manner with the next two stanzas of the poem. She models problem solving two additional tricky by asking herself questions.
Teacher: *Well, now that I finished reading this poem, I am asking myself, "Did this make sense to me with what I know about birthdays?"*	
Well, I think it's kind of silly to have a birthday cake that grows larger every year, although that could be fun! I now understand why it would be a cake big enough for a giant after several birthdays!	At the end of the poem, the teacher is connecting information from the poem to reflect on its meaning.

3. Collaborative use of the strategy in action:

Teacher: *Did you notice how I asked myself questions to make sure I always understood what I was reading? Let's try this again with a new piece of text.*	Teacher is beginning to invite students to participate in the lesson.
Open your books to page 38. What kind of before reading questions should we ask ourselves that will help us get a focus for reading and help us see if we can figure out what this might be about?	
Student 1: *I think it is about swimming.*	
Teacher: *How can we turn that into a question that you might ask before you get started with reading?*	
Student 1: *What is this about?*	
Teacher: *Let's write that down because that's a great question that readers ask before they get started to focus their attention to start trying to figure out what will make sense. Anything else?*	Teacher writes question on chart paper.
Student 2: *I am asking . . . (reads aloud title—"A Real Winner") what did he win?"*	Teacher writes question on chart paper.
Teacher: *Another good question that comes from reading the title. Thinking of questions about the title helps you focus on your reading because now you want to read to find answers to the questions, yes? C., what questions are coming to your mind as you look through all the pages?*	The teacher is closely guiding students as they attempt to identify important information on a short section of text. By raising questions and asking students to explain their responses, she is monitoring their understanding of the skill and strategy.
Student 3: *I am wondering how long is it?*	
Teacher: *Another question a skillful reader might ask, because you want to know how much time it might take you to read, right?*	

(Continued)

Example 5.1 (Continued)

Let's get started reading. How about T. reading the first page.	
Student 4 reads aloud up to the last word on the page. He stops. . . . There is a long pause.	Teacher waits because student is obviously cognitively engaged and trying to sort out his response. Other students know not to interrupt his "think time."
Teacher: *Why did you stop, T.?*	
Student 4: *Because I don't know that word.*	
Teacher: *T., what questions can you ask, or anyone else, that might help T. figure out this tricky word? Remember some of the questions I asked when I encountered a tricky word reading the poem.*	Teacher reminds students about the questions she modeled.
Student 3: *Do you know any chunks?*	
Teacher: *I am going to add that to our chart of questions that help us self-regulate because that's a question a reader should ask to help figure out unknown words.* *T., did asking this question help you look through the word?*	
Student 4: *Yes, I see the word "ships."*	
Teacher: *Another question you might ask is, "Will rereading the sentence and thinking about what might make sense help?" Go ahead and try . . .*	
Student 4 rereads the sentence and again stops at the word . . . then begins sounding out the word, Ch . . . ch . . . am . . . ships . . . and correctly says, *championships!*	
Teacher: *Nice job problem solving! Will you reread the sentence quickly and then think aloud what was going on in your head that helped you fix up your reading.*	Teacher asks student to explain his thinking to make sure he understands and to allow others to hear his explanation.
Student 4 rereads.	
Student 4: *I was thinking about the other words, "Can she help the team win the . . . " and then I thought of championships.*	
Teacher: *Does everyone agree "championships" makes sense?*	
All five students show thumbs up.	
Teacher: *And you could check that you were right because "championships" makes sense and it ends in the chunk you said you know, "ships," correct?*	

Student 4: *Yes.*	
Teacher: *Let's work on the next page together also.*	Teacher makes a decision to continue in the collaborative step with the next page so she can involve more students and check their understanding.
4. Guided practice using the strategy with gradual release of responsibility:	
Teacher: *You did a great job with that page and we added another question to our chart: What would I say if I were talking? That is another question readers use when they come across a tricky word, because reading is a lot like talk written down.* *Let's turn the page but before we read, is there a question we might want to ask that would help us self-regulate or keep track of our reading?*	The teacher now begins to step back and let students become more responsible for using the skill.
Student 2: *Is that little kid in the picture Janet?*	
Teacher: *That is a good self-regulating question, because it will help us keep track of the main character. I definitely need to write this one down so we can remember to use it again. I am going to write the question so we can use it with many different books—does the picture/illustration give me information that helps me keep track of my reading?* *Now I'd like everyone to whisper read while I come and listen in on each of you. When I come to you, let me know the questions and the thinking you are doing to help you keep track of your reading . . .*	As the teacher rotates listening in with each reader, she records their reading accuracy and makes notes of the questions they pose. She reinforces how asking questions helps a reader self-regulate and make sure reading is making sense.
5. Independent use of the strategy:	
Teacher: *Today we tried asking questions that would help us make sure we are self-regulating our reading. Why is it important to self-regulate?*	The teacher closes the lesson by reinforcing how asking questions helps a reader self-regulate. The independent step of the lesson is structured so that students can provide support to each other if needed. The final question moves students to a next level of work: how questions about background knowledge support self-regulating.
Student 3: *Because we need to make sure everything makes sense.*	
Teacher: *Exactly! And thinking of questions is one way to help us to keep checking on our reading as we try to find answers to our questions.* *I would like you now to go to a quiet space in the room.*	

Example 5.1 (Continued)

Teacher partners two students and puts the other three together. Teacher: *Quietly read the last two pages and if you come to a tricky word or confusing spot, I want your partner(s) to ask you questions that might help you fix up the problem.* *At the end of the reading, I want each of you to ask yourself the question I wrote on this paper: "How does this story about Janet Evans fit in with what I know about trying to reach a goal?" Talk about your answer with each other and explain your thinking. We'll continue to talk about self-regulating tomorrow. Nice job everyone!*	Students are expected to independently extend what they learned about the role of questioning in the strategy self-regulating. By putting the lesson objective into practice, students are on their way to becoming responsible for ensuring their reading makes sense and fixing it when it doesn't. Subsequent lessons, across a variety of genre, will integrate other skills that are embedded in the strategy self-regulating. Additionally, small group and whole class lessons will reinforce self-regulating in other learning tasks.

Here is a peek at another small group reading lesson focusing on self-regulating in a Grade 6 classroom. This teacher found her students needed to be more willing to recognize comprehension problems, after observing the students in a small group lesson during a recent science class. They were very reluctant to seek help even when it was clear they had become lost in the science text. The lesson below reflects the first lesson in self-regulating.

Example 5.2   Small Group Reading Lesson

Strategy: Self-Regulating.	Comprehension strategy emphasized during this lesson.
Focus Skills: Rereading and reading ahead.	Skills that support self-regulating and will be the teaching point for the lesson.
Instructional Activity: Discussion and think-aloud.	
Lesson Design:	The following five steps make up the lesson procedure.
1. Explicit description of the strategy—when the strategy should be used: Teacher: *Yesterday afternoon we had some reading to do from our science textbook. It was a pretty challenging chapter to read, wasn't it?* Student 1: *Yes, and I didn't get it at all.* Teacher: *Yes, I noticed you had trouble, but there are things that we can do as readers that will help us. . . . We know good readers are always self-regulating . . . making sure reading makes sense and fixing it when it doesn't.*	Clear description of the strategy and skill that will be taught in the lesson.

Rereading and reading ahead are important fix-up skills that can help us get back on track after we realize things are not making sense. That's what we are going to do today.	Rereading is often independent readers' *first* response to solving problems in text while struggling readers rarely consider going back.
Student 3: *Why would I reread the same stuff when it didn't make sense the first time?*	
Teacher: *Great question. Sometimes rereading is not enough, but by rereading and reading ahead, we can often figure things out. Let's see as we work through this quick lesson together.*	

2. Teacher and/or student modeling of the strategy in action:

Teacher: *I'll start by reading this short article I found in the newspaper last night. I clipped this out because I have been following Barbaro's progress after watching him (on television) tragically break his leg in the Preakness Stakes—the big horse race. The headline says, "Concern for Barbaro."*	The text selected for modeling is short and involves a topic that the students have been following in the news and are very interested in.
Teacher starts reading.	
Teacher: *"A custom-made cast was removed and Barbaro underwent a procedure on his right hind leg, the same leg the Kentucky Derby winner shattered eight months ago in the Preakness."*	
Boy that was a long sentence! Right now, I am not sure I understand which leg the cast came off—was it his right leg? The one that underwent a procedure? I am going to reread this paragraph because I am not sure.	Teacher models the strategy by thinking aloud as she reads.
Teacher rereads.	
Teacher: *You know, this is still unclear to me, but I think I need to read on and see if I get more information.*	Teacher acknowledges her continued confusion and explains why she decided to read ahead.
Teacher continues.	
Teacher: *"It is the first time in weeks the right hind leg has been the focus of concern. 'They did some procedures on the one he originally injured,' co-owner Roy Jackson told the Associated Press. 'He's got a lot of issues, and not any of them is bad enough to say goodbye. But, put together, it's not a good day for Barbaro.'"*	
I am looking back at the first sentence in this paragraph . . .	

(Continued)

Example 5.2 (Continued)

Teacher rereads.	
Teacher: *"It is the first time in weeks the right hind leg has been the focus of concern."*	
In rereading this, I am thinking that the cast must have come off of his other leg because they haven't been concerned about his right leg for weeks. The writer still hasn't been very clear about communicating this. . . . I'll keep going.	Teacher thinks aloud and explains why she went back.
"This is the first time in weeks the right hind leg has been the focus of concern. For months, it was the left hind leg that put Barbaro's recovery in serious jeopardy because of laminitis, the often-fatal hoof disease."	The confusion is beginning to be resolved but the teacher lets the students know that the writing is not very clear. Struggling readers rarely consider that the way the text is written may be contributing to their comprehension difficulties.
Ahh . . . now I have confirmation both his right and left hind legs have had major problems . . . hmmm, now that I know this I am going to go back and reread the article from the beginning and focus on finding out how Barbaro is doing . . .	Teacher reflects how the new information further clarified her confusion.
Teacher quickly rereads.	
Teacher: *Well, it seems as soon as Barbaro gets one thing fixed, he develops another serious problem. I now understand the writer is telling us that when you put all these problems together, Barbaro is still in serious shape. I had to reread and read ahead to sort everything out, but now I understand. Sometimes I paused after one sentence, didn't I? Sometimes I looped back after I read ahead for a bit, and at the end, when things were clearer, I reread the whole thing to make sure I could put it all together. This is our job as readers who self-regulate!*	Teacher explains how rereading and reading ahead helped her make sense of this article. Teacher clearly restates how rereading and reading ahead help a reader keep track of comprehension.
3. Collaborative use of the strategy in action:	
Teacher: *Now, I want you to go back to the pages you read in your science book yesterday.*	
Students groan.	
Teacher: *Well, we know we can't just continue on when things are not making sense. So, let's first talk about where your confusion started. C., look over the first page and find the point where you started getting confused.*	Teacher is still keeping a close watch over students as they begin to practice. The teacher needs to be absolutely sure students are successful in their skill practice before releasing them to practice on their own.

Student 1: *Here, in the third sentence. . . .* (Student reads sentence aloud.) *This just doesn't make sense.* **Teacher:** *Anyone else confused by this sentence?* Students 2 and 3 both nod. **Student 2:** *I didn't get it because . . . I don't understand what it means to ti- ti-titrate something . . . acid.*	The fact the student can identify the point of confusion is valuable information for the teacher. If the student didn't know where his reading broke down, the lesson would have taken a different direction.
Teacher: *Okay, go back and try rereading from the beginning. Now that you have a focus for reading—you want to find out what it means to titrate an acid—reread the first part.* **Student 1:** *"In the laboratory, scientists do a special kind of neutralization experiment, called a titration. Scientists use a titration to identify the strength of an unknown acid or base. To titrate an acid, they add small amounts of a base and check the pH after every addition . . ."*	Teacher points out that a reader has a specific purpose in mind when he/she goes back to reread.
Teacher: *I noticed something you did as you reread . . . you slowed down your reading because you are now very focused on what you are searching for. Let's stop at the first sentence.* Teacher rereads.	Teacher points out another self-regulating skill being integrated with rereading (change in reading rate). Teacher signals to students that the idea is important.
Teacher: *What is the author telling us about titration?* **Student 3:** *It is the name of a special kind of experiment.*	The teacher is turning the thinking back to the students with this question.
Teacher: *Did the author tell us any more about titration in this first sentence?* **Student 2:** *It is a* (reads from book) *neutralization experiment.* **Student 1:** *Neutral like we did the other day when we looked at things that were neither acid nor alkaline and then some that were.*	The teacher is probing for a more in-depth answer.
Teacher: *Nice connecting! Yes, so in rereading this section and sentence, you noticed you do know something about experiments that the author is writing about. Read the second sentence again.* Students reread.	In commenting and paraphrasing, the teacher is marking the importance of what the student did as a reader so it will be noticed by all students.
Teacher: *What is the author telling us in this second sentence?*	The teacher is keeping the students aware of how rereading is helping them better understand.

(Continued)

Example 5.2 (Continued)

Student 1: *This experiment can identify the strength of an unknown acid or base.*	
Teacher: *Exactly! So, each time you are rereading you have gotten a better sense of what the author is trying to say . . . that there is a certain type of experiment, called titration, that identifies how strong an acid or base is.* *We are up to the third sentence. C., want to reread it now?*	The teacher is recapping what the student did while rereading in order to encourage the students to continue to practice rereading.
Student 1: (rereads) *Okay, now I get it . . . to titrate is to do this kind of experiment . . . to keep adding base and checking, adding more and rechecking.*	
Teacher: *Kind of what you are doing as a reader! You got confused, you went back, reread, thought about it, reread a little more, and by the time you came to the part you weren't sure about, you had a better sense of what the author was talking about. Nice job! Putting it all together confirmed that this now makes sense.* *Let's try another part where you were confused.*	The teacher carefully walks students through another example so she can collect more information about how students are doing.
4. Guided practice using the strategy with gradual release of responsibility:	
Teacher: *Now I want you to look over the next page. Reread the page. If there is a point where you are confused, put a light pencil check next to it. Then, go back at least to the beginning of the paragraph and reread to see if that will help. Remember, you may also need to read ahead a little if rereading doesn't clarify all your confusion, but don't keep going too long if you are still confused.* *I will be checking in with each of you before you go back to your seats.*	As the teacher checks in with each reader, she continually assesses each student's progress by asking probing questions and having students think aloud.
5. Independent use of the strategy:	
Teacher: *Each of you did a great job of rereading and reading ahead in a couple of cases. Remember, readers need to do this all the time as part of monitoring their understanding. Let's talk about some of the reasons rereading helped you just now. What did we talk about that I noticed you doing when I was listening in with each of you rereading your pages just now?*	Because the teacher is confident that the three students are able to use the skills rereading and reading ahead, she is ready to send them back to their seats for independent practice. Although this science book is written at a fairly easy level for sixth grade, the information is

Student 1: *I slowed down when I reread the sentence again.*	sometimes too dense for the struggling readers. By breaking it down and rereading/reading ahead, the students learned how to fix up their confusion.
Teacher: *Yes, and how did that help?*	The teacher has the students help her recap the reasons why rereading helped them better comprehend by articulating exactly what the skill did for them as readers.
Student 1: *It made my mind slow down and think more about each word.*	
Teacher: *Excellent. T.?*	
Student 3: *I knew what parts I understood so I could read those parts quicker.*	
Teacher: *Yes, by reading through the easier parts quickly, you saved energy for the trouble spots. You also reflected on the information in the easy parts to see if that could help you with the hard parts, right?*	
Student 2: *I was thinking more about what didn't make sense when I reread.*	
Teacher: *Right, rereading and thinking about the confusing part didn't feel as overwhelming as trying to think about everything at once. These are all good reasons to reread and/or read ahead. We will talk about this more tomorrow.*	
You read these pages once yesterday and didn't understand them very well, did you? So if you were going to give yourself a score of 1 to 3 for yesterday's understanding of these pages, it would probably be a 1. (3 means you understood very well; 2 means you understood most of it; 1 means you are confused.) I want you to read these pages one more time before we meet tomorrow. Give yourself an understanding point of 1, 2, or 3 after you finish rereading and see if your score changes. If you practice what we talked about today, I know you will do this well!	The independent activity is intended to motivate students to improve their score. The teacher will check the accuracy of their self-regulating tomorrow.

Often, content area reading is completed as a whole class lesson. Supporting all readers in the class while still getting through the information that needs to be covered becomes a real challenge for teachers. Publishers too frequently jam a lot of complex and important information into a small amount of text. These texts can be up to three years above the average students' reading level and cover a breadth of concepts with little reader support provided. If saddled with such inappropriate content area textbooks, many teachers are very resourceful in finding supplemental materials that help address the range of students' reading levels. The lesson design, however, is also critical to reaching all students.

SELF-REGULATING ACROSS CONTENT AREAS

Below is a snapshot of one teacher's attempt to ensure all students in his classroom learn the important text concepts during this whole group science lesson. The lesson uses a seventh grade science class. The six students who struggle with reading were highly engaged and successful with the lab investigations they completed with their partners the previous day. These at-risk readers would have had a difficult time reading the directions for their lab investigation if the teacher had not paired each with a more capable reader as a lab partner. As the class begins a new unit, the teacher does not want text readability to hold any of his students back from learning the seventh grade science concepts they are so excited about. Previously, he and the building reading consultant have had conversations about how to address his concern. She suggested using an instructional practice called Questioning the Author (QtA) (Beck, McKeown, Hamilton, & Kucan, 1997). The science teacher then invited the building reading consultant in to help him launch QtA.

Example 5.3   Whole Group Seventh Grade Science Lesson

Strategy: Self-Regulating.	Comprehension strategy emphasized during this lesson.
Focus Skill: Questioning the author.	
Lesson Design:	The following five steps make up the lesson procedure and gradually release responsibility for reading work from the teacher to the students.
1. Explicit description of the strategy—when the strategy should be used:	
Teacher: *Okay, I recognize that reading our science textbooks can be difficult, but we need to use our textbooks to help us build the background knowledge necessary for our lab investigations. So, today I would like to introduce a practice that I expect we will use frequently as we read chapters from our science text.* *Mrs. L. is here to help us learn a new way of thinking about science reading. I expect you will give her your full attention as she walks us through this process. Mrs. L.*	Teacher gives a clear description of what the class will be doing and connects the lesson's expectations to previous learning.
Mrs. L.: *Hi everyone! I'm excited to work with you and Mr. H. today. First, before we get started, I need to have you rearrange your desks so everyone is in a large U and can see everyone else's face. Let me see how quickly and quietly we can accomplish this. . . .*	QtA uses discussion as a context to encourage students to collaborate to construct meaning, so a classroom arrangement that encourages dialogue is being used.

Students and teacher move quickly to rearrange their seats.	
Mrs. L.: *Great! Thanks for your help, Mr. H.*	
We are going to use a different type of reading from what you might be used to. An important idea to remember when reading your science book, or any book for that matter, is that writers, or authors, are real people, and just like you and me, they are not perfect. Sometimes authors are experts in a subject, such as science, but they may not always write or explain things in a way that makes it easy for readers to figure out.	Students are introduced to the notion that authors are not perfect. This is an important message, especially to the struggling readers who assume they are always at fault when they do not comprehend text. The point is to bolster their willingness to reveal when the text is difficult to understand and to recognize it may not be their fault.
2. Teacher and/or student modeling of the strategy in action:	
Mrs. L.: *Open your books to the beginning of Chapter 3 and let me show you how QtA, Question-the-Author, works. You listen while I model.*	In preparing for this lesson, the classroom teacher and the reading consultant (Mrs. L.) read and anticipated the potential problems in the text (lack of clarity, density of information, etc.) that might interfere with students' understanding.
Mrs. L. reads aloud the title, and tells students she is scanning the whole page, and then she begins reading aloud.	
Mrs. L.: *"A forest is filled with an amazing variety of living things. Some are easy to see, but you have to look closely to find others. If you look carefully at the floor of the forest, you can often find spots of bright color."*	
Mrs. L. stops reading to think aloud.	
Mrs. L: *I never heard of "the floor of a forest." Hmm, I wonder why the author used that word? I guess it means the ground that you walk on, since I walk on the floor in a building. . . . I think the author is trying to be fancy in his language. I think the author is trying to tell me the ground is like a floor in a forest . . . the author is making me do a little work here.*	Reading consultant models the questions she would ask the author when reading is difficult. When preparing a traditional content area text lesson, teachers often do not consider the author's intent or meaning.
Mrs. L. continues to read.	
Mrs. L: *"If you look carefully at the floor of a forest, you can often find spots of bright color. A beautiful pink coral fungus grows beneath tall trees."*	
Pink coral? Wow! I know coral grows in the ocean but I didn't know it grows in a forest. I am going back to the picture I looked at before I started reading. I want to reread the caption by the picture of the pink coral. . . . I am asking myself, "Why is the author telling me this?"	When using QtA, the text is not considered a source of fixed or constructed information. The emphasis on author awareness helps students and teachers bring the writer into the forefront and points out how the writer can make understanding hard or easy on the reader.
Mrs. L. continues her think-aloud for the next three sentences, which takes her to the bottom of the page.	
Mrs. L.: *Did anyone see anything else confusing as you were reading along?*	

(Continued)

Example 5.3 (Continued)

Student 1: *I get confused about all the boxes and other stuff on the page.*	
Mrs. L.: *That's a really good point. Sometimes writers try to put so much information on the page it gets confusing about what to read first. What would you do instead?*	
Student 1: *I'd put everything but the picture and the words on another page. Maybe I would number stuff like, read number 1 first, read number 2 second . . .*	
Mrs. L.: *I like that. It would help give us direction as a reader. So you have a suggestion for how the author could organize the information in a way that would make the reading clearer to you. You could do that you know. You could make a plan about what you are going to read first, next, and so on.*	
The point is, we as readers have to recognize that authors don't always write or organize information in the clearest way, so we, as readers, need to figure out how to make it clear to us. Here are some questions we can ask the author when we are reading—as if the author were sitting here with us. Here they are . . .	
Mrs. L. writes on the board:	
What is the author trying to tell us? *Why is the author telling us that?* *Is it said clearly?* *How might the author have written it more clearly?* *What would you have wanted to say instead?*	
3. Collaborative use of the strategy in action:	
Teacher: *We are going to use these questions as we continue to read. Turn to page 51.*	QtA differs from other self-regulation questions because (in this lesson) it emphasizes the fallibility of an author. Students are prompted to react to text in a different way by grappling with how the author's ideas might be expressed in a clearer way. The discussion is not the goal of QtA, rather discussion in a QtA lesson is a means of achieving the goal of constructing meaning from the text.
Teacher reads aloud the first paragraph.	
Teacher: *"An Overview of Cells. You are made up of cells. Cells are the basic units of structure and function in living things. This means cells form the parts of an organism and carry out all of an organism's processes or functions."*	
Mrs. L.: *Hold on; I'm wondering about these sentences. What is the author trying to tell us here? We have some terms piling up.*	
Student 2: *Cells are, umm, important.*	Student is mainly focusing on one word. The teacher persists in trying to get the students to reach greater meaning.
Mrs. L.: *Okay, but I am still a little confused . . .*	

Silence for many seconds.	Teacher gives plenty of time for students to process.
Student 2: *Well, cells are part of every living thing . . . and they carry out all the functions.*	
Teacher: *Can you add more, T.? Can you tell us what the author wanted us to know more clearly, in your own words as if you were writing this?*	Teacher expects student to student dialogue and is still pushing students to explain more in their own words.
Student 2: *The author is trying to let us know that cells are part of every living thing and they do stuff to keep us alive.*	
Teacher: *So you said the author is telling us about the importance of cells and what they do. Those are really good ideas. Do you think you made the information clearer when T. restated it?*	Teacher recaps the ideas and points out that they, not the author, made the information more understandable.
	The teacher now moves to applying the concept to more text reading. Asking a student to begin by reading the next section orally allows the teacher to stay closely involved before releasing more responsibility to the students.
Students: *Yes.*	
4. Guided practice using the strategy with gradual release of responsibility:	
Mrs. L.: *Let's have S. read the next section aloud. While she is reading, keep asking yourself, "What does the author mean here?" "Does the author explain this clearly?"*	Classroom teacher and reading consultant continue to press students with questions to assess their progress.
As the discussion of the remaining two sections on this page continues, the teachers assist students in integrating and connecting ideas, and they focus on student understanding.	
Teacher: *Now we'd like you to read the next two pages silently. When you are finished, we'll talk together and see if we have figured out what the author is trying to say and whether or not the information could be stated more clearly.*	Both the reading consultant and the teacher randomly confer one-on-one with students to closely monitor their progress.
5. Independent use of the strategy:	
Teacher: *This chapter was packed with information. One of the most important points in this chapter that we discovered is the cell theory. Let's look back at the board at what we said the author was trying to tell us about cell theory.*	Teacher is revoicing and recapping the highlights of the lesson content.
Teacher points back to the key points about cell theory written on the board.	

(Continued)

Example 5.3 (Continued)

Teacher:	*Yet, we discovered that the author jammed a whole bunch of other information in this chapter about different types of microscopes, their magnification, scientists, and how they used the microscopes to advance the cell theory . . . and cell theory is mentioned rather incidentally. Mrs. L. showed us that authors don't always explain things well, so we have to work to make sure we understand what we are reading.*	Teacher reiterates how authors don't always make it easy for readers to make sense of text.
Mrs. L.:	*After your first-draft reading of this chapter with a lot of questions that helped you monitor your understanding, do you have a better sense of the important information the author wanted us to know?*	
Students nod in agreement.		
Teacher:	*Tonight for homework, I want you to go back and write in your own words what the main ideas the author wanted you to know about cell theory. You are the author this time. We'll pick up there tomorrow. Nice job folks! And thanks Mrs. L. We'll have you back again.*	The homework assignment will provide the teachers with an assessment of those students who may still be grappling with understanding.

CONCLUSIONS AND REFLECTIONS

Too often it becomes easy for a disengaged reader to lose track of monitoring comprehension. I liken this behavior to times I turn on the television to catch the weather forecast and miss the whole thing. Even though I am staring at the screen, I suddenly realize the newscaster is signing off for the evening, "Well that's it for tonight!" Anyone observing would think I was paying attention. I had a clear purpose for listening, and my ears heard the weather forecaster talking, but nothing registered; I was completely detached!

With printed text, we have the opportunity to recover and go back when we notice our attention drift away from creating meaning. Struggling readers need to learn that one of their primary jobs is to be actively involved with monitoring text and in adjusting when meaning is confusing or lost. By teaching self-regulating skills across many different types of text, we can begin to help readers change their belief that comprehension problems are beyond their reach.

Self-regulated readers have a repertoire of skills they apply appropriately to tackle the challenges of difficult and complex text. With self-regulation comes a deeper understanding of subject matter and greater success. This explains why self-regulating promotes a high sense of reader self-efficacy.

Readers' Questions and Author's Answers

Q: How long should instruction remain on each strategy?

A: Teachers often spend three to five weeks on a strategy, but the best answer is to spend enough time to be confident your students deeply understand how the focus strategy works. Students need to have ample experiences practicing the strategy across a variety of text types and in texts that gradually increase in reading difficulty. Students should also have numerous lessons practicing many of the skills embedded in the focus strategy. As more responsibility for strategic reading is released from the teacher to the student, there should be a generous amount of data (i.e., teacher observations, students' verbal explanations of their thinking, performance on independent tasks, etc.) that clearly show students' increased awareness of the connections among strategies and understanding of each.

Q: Won't students get bored spending so much time on one strategy?

A: They really don't! I believe part of the reason students stay engaged is that they are finally experiencing success with reading and success is a great motivator. Second, they are practicing strategies and supporting skills across a variety of interesting texts. Selecting the appropriate texts is essential.

This chapter showed how to deliberately pull apart the strategy self-regulating so that it can be explicitly taught to struggling readers. Chapter 6 will explore another important comprehension strategy—*inferring.*

6

Putting the Strategies Into Practice

Inferring

To push beyond the literal text, to make it personal and three dimensional, to weave it into our own stories—that is to infer.

—Keene and Zimmermann (1997)

As we know, the world is a complicated place where many things spoken, viewed, and written are neither clearly right or wrong, nor black or white. Rather, there is a lot of gray area for us to contend with, and in order to do so, we learn how to infer. Inferring is necessary to successfully navigate our way in the world. We infer that winter is coming as we observe the fall leaves and temperatures drop. As we stroll down the sidewalk, we note the smells emanating from our favorite restaurant and we infer the chef must be preparing for the dinner crowd. When we read about a character's actions, we infer what kind of person he or she is.

When we react to our observations (e.g., draw a conclusion or offer an explanation about what is implied), we are making an inference. The strategy *inferring* attempts to explain or catalog or speculate the information we read or observe. In reading, inferring is also a basic survival strategy, for it helps unlock and personalize that which the author has not made explicit.

KEY TERMINOLOGY

Inferring: This strategy involves seeing and considering ideas that are not literally on the printed page.

- **Using background knowledge:** The importance of the background knowledge a reader brings to text became recognized in what is known as schema theory. Reading is now understood to be an active process of constructing meaning by connecting one's own knowledge and prior experiences with the information found in text.
- **Determining author's purpose:** Determining an author's purpose is identifying the reason or reasons an author wrote a selection.
- **Being aware of text language:** The literary techniques that an author uses often help a reader visualize ideas and make connections, but they also require a reader to infer the meaning behind the words.
- **Recognizing author's biases/views:** Learning to identify the ways an author may manipulate data or expose strong feelings for or against a character, group, or issue supports the ability to infer. Thoughtful readers learn to decipher what is implied or suggested just as well as what is explicitly stated and to separate fact from opinion.
- **Making predictions:** The subtle clues the author offers trigger predictions about meaning, outcomes, actions of characters, events of a plot, and resolutions of problems. In informational text, features such as bold headings, illustrations, or side notes can be used to predict information that is significant.
- **Determining theme:** The skill of determining theme means a reader must identify the central (and possibly minor) lesson or moral about life, the nature of man, or the world that was developed in the selection.
- **Drawing conclusions:** This skill refers to a reader arriving at a logical decision or opinion based on information presented in a text (implied and explicit) combined with the background knowledge and experiences of the reader.
- **Questioning:** Questions that support the strategy inferring include: *What conclusion can I draw based on the ideas presented? What opinions are revealed in the selection? Where can I find clues about the character's feelings? What information is missing? Based on what I've read so far and what I know about this topic, what might come next? How can I use my questions to modify the emerging theme? What is this figurative language really implying?*
- **Synthesizing text clues and various types of connections:** A reader using this skill fills in details and information about what the writer is implying based on their text connections (text-to-self, text-to-text, or text-to-world).

WHAT IS INFERRING?

Chapter 1 explained how readers make inferences by constructing meaning from the information provided in the text (text-based inference) and by using the information they bring to the text from their background experiences (knowledge-based inference). In both cases, the reader is interacting with the text. Rosenblatt (1978) and Iser (1978) called this direct exchange of meaning between the reader and the text transactional theory.

The reader who struggles with comprehension is often not able to fulfill a transactional role with text. Rather, he or she expects the text to supply everything. Iser (1978) tells us that were text to offer everything, the reader would be bored and dissatisfied. As readers, our imagination and intellect must have work to do, details to sketch in, implications to elaborate, and/or questions to answer—otherwise reading would be a monotonous and unchallenging activity. The inferring strategy requires this kind of mindful work. Yet, too often we are quick to put struggling readers in low-readability texts that have controlled vocabulary, a high level of predictability, and leave little to the imagination. Thus, we inadvertently contribute to these students' aversion to reading and to their dependency on literal level understanding. In turn, if a text demands too much and offers too little, even with attempts to infer meaning, the text can overstrain and frustrate any reader. Keene and Zimmermann (1997) tell us inferring has many facets and great books provoke us to consider and use them all.

Authors skillfully provide some information directly and insinuate or imply other information. If in the process of reading, we are mindful of the fluctuations we go through—changing perspectives, revising impressions, passing through a series of emotional states, discovering new insights—we begin to see the amount of inferring we are doing. Inferring, according to Anderson and Pearson (1984), is the heart of meaning construction for learners of all ages. Inferring is essential to comprehension and for this reason was selected as one of the Four Powerful Comprehension Strategies.

WHEN DOES A READER INFER?

An oversimplified answer to this question is that a reader infers every time he or she makes an educated "guess" about the meaning of text. This does not mean a random, off the wall guess, but one that is grounded in the information presented and the reader's background knowledge. In order to infer, a reader needs to integrate and apply a variety of the skills that are embedded in this complex strategy. A sentence as simple as, "She bowed her head, took a deep breath, and allowed the stillness to wash over her," can evoke a range of conclusions based on a reader's inference. For example, a reader may infer the person is an elderly person who is in church. Another may infer the person is a young woman starting a yoga lesson. A third reader may infer it is a little girl who just entered the refuge of her secret hiding place away from her loud and tormenting brothers. The examples go on and on. Each example shows how several inferences were made in an attempt to make sense of the text. Some of the inferences come from the information that the author supplied in the text. For example, the pronoun "she" has no antecedent, but an assumption can be made that this woman or girl is an important character. Further, some of the inferences come from the reader's background knowledge. For example, bowing one's head is a behavior typically associated with prayer, meditation, and/or relief.

A skillful reader infers when trying to figure out explanations about why events are occurring; why characters behave and interact as they do; why the author chose to write the text; and why a particular setting was selected for the story. The strategy of inferring is also at work when a search is made for context clues to unlock an unknown word; when a reader tries to connect antecedents and pronouns; and when readers link different elements of text. Making predictions is a form of inferring (Keene & Zimmermann, 1997), because predictions also require a reader to combine background knowledge with information presented in the text to draw conclusions. A prediction, however, can either be confirmed or rejected as the reader reads further, but inferences can be left to the reader's imagination or judgment. Many books lend themselves to great debates among readers as to their "real" meaning and this is what makes them so memorable and interesting to read and discuss!

WHY DO READERS INFER?

Good readers infer in order to connect with, make sense of, and appreciate text to the fullest extent. Inferring is the defining strategy that separates independent readers from struggling readers (Oczkus, 2004). Readers infer differently depending on their purpose for reading. For example, if a reader is reading informational text (a research study) with the purpose of learning about an unfamiliar topic, more text-based inferences will probably be used to support comprehension. The reader will most likely be making predictions, generating questions, connecting different sections of the research, and drawing conclusions based on the information presented by the author. If, however, a reader is reading a novel for enjoyment, inferences are more likely to be shaped by the reader's knowledge of the world. The reader will need to draw from personal experiences to fully connect with the book and to appreciate the emotions of a character. Inferring is just the beginning.

Why is inferring such an important comprehension strategy? Because inferring allows a new layer of the reader's personality to be brought to light; Iser (1978) believes the significance of the work does not [just] lie in the meaning sealed within the text, but in the fact that that meaning brings out what had previously been sealed within us. How great is that?

SAMPLE LESSONS FOR THE STRATEGY INFERRING

Background: The following is a description of a fourth grade small group reading lesson, taking place early in the school year. This example may help demonstrate how the five steps of a gradual release small group reading comprehension lesson look in practice. The teacher designed the lesson around previously identified student needs, with four students participating in this reading group. At the start of the new school year, all were reading approximately one year below the typical reader in this fourth grade classroom.

Important note: This lesson example is not intended to be scripted instruction. The Gradual Release Lesson Procedure (Chapter 2) is intended to show how lessons need to explicitly teach comprehension strategies; however, the effectiveness of the lesson hinges on the teacher's ability to make decisions based on how students respond. This is one of the many strategy lessons that might be used to teach the various skills of inferring across different types of texts.

Example 6.1 Small Group Reading Lesson

Strategy: Inferring.	Comprehension strategy emphasized during this lesson.
Focus Skill: Making predictions.	Through previous assessments, the teacher identified the need for these students to make better use of predictions to help them infer.
Instructional Activity/Technique: Group chart and discussion.	Chart paper was used to record students' predictions and to facilitate discussion.
Lesson Design:	The following five steps make up the lesson procedure.
1. Explicit description of the strategy—when the strategy should be used: Teacher writes word on chart paper: *Inference* Teacher: *I'll bet everyone here knows what this means.* Students shake their heads no. Teacher: *Okay, watch me.* Teacher gives nonverbal cue—makes a sad face. Teacher: *If you see someone who looks like this, what would you think?* Students: (yelling out) *They are sad!* Teacher: *Did I tell you I was sad?* Student 1: *No! But that's the face my baby brother makes when he is ready to start crying.* Teacher: *You used what you have learned, that people who look like this are feeling sad, and even though I didn't say I was sad, you were able to figure out I was feeling sad. You made an inference!* *Good readers make inferences before they begin reading and while they are reading. An inference is taking information that an author writes about in a book and adding your own knowledge to it. Just like*	Some teachers worry that students will not understand strategy terms, such as inference. More often than not, students will not be confused by correct terminology if instruction is at the appropriate level for the students, the students are given many opportunities to successfully use the strategy across a variety of texts, and the lesson activities clearly exemplify the strategy being taught.

(Continued)

Example 6.1 (Continued)

you took information about the face I was making and used it with what you know about how people feel when they look like this. *There are many ways a reader makes an inference. One way is by making predictions . . .* Teacher writes out word on chart paper: *Predictions* Teacher: *. . . just as you did a minute ago.* *Predicting is thinking about what is going to happen next based on what you think the author is trying to tell you and on what you know from your background experiences. So, you might predict that I was going to cry, just like your baby brother does when he makes such a face, right?* *When reading stories, good readers make predictions about how the story is going to go— from the book title, the pictures, the words in the story, and many other sources of information. Readers then read on to see if their predictions are correct. If they aren't, they change them. Making predictions helps you make inferences, because you are thinking about what might happen next.*	
2. Teacher and/or student modeling of the strategy in action:	
Teacher: *Let me show you. I am going to make predictions while I read this book. I'll start with the cover. Hmm . . . I see a picture of a whale. It looks kind of like a cartoon character. I predict* (points to the word on chart paper) *that this is going to be a make-believe or fiction story because I don't think a whale smiles like this. The title will give me more clues about the book. The title is* IBIS: A True Whale Story. *Yikes, my prediction was not correct! I need to change it. This is a true story. The illustrator just chose to use a picture that looks like a cartoon. I've made some predictions about the book from the cover, and now I'll start reading.*	Teacher models the strategy by thinking aloud. Notice, teacher has control over the lesson, but students could be invited to participate in this phase of the lesson if the teacher is confident they can participate in the modeling correctly.
3. Collaborative use of the strategy in action:	
Teacher: *Okay, I want you to make predictions with me. Each of us should stop when we think we have a prediction. Let's read this page together.* *Can anyone make a prediction on this page?*	Teacher is beginning to invite students to take some control over the lesson.

Student 1: (points to the word "pod") *What does pod mean?*	
Teacher: *What information could we use to help us figure this out?*	Predicting at the word level is also a skill that supports the strategy self-regulating.
Student 3: *We could use the picture.*	
Teacher: *What information would you use in the picture?*	
Student: *Well, there are a bunch of whales together . . .*	
Teacher: *Do you think pod could be another word for a group of whales?*	The teacher brings students back to making predictions about the upcoming story line.
Students nod.	
Teacher: *Let's think about what we have read so far that may help us predict what is going to happen next in this book.*	
Student: *Well, Ibis must be a special whale since this book is about him and not all the other whales.*	
Teacher: *Is there a sentence that you have read so far that says there is something special about Ibis?*	
Students: (after scanning page) *No.*	
Teacher: *So, you are using the title of this book plus the information we have read so far to make a prediction about what we may learn as we read further. That is excellent!*	Teacher recaps students' thinking to ensure students understand how the prediction was made.
Teacher continues having students read orally and discusses with them another prediction that comes up.	
4. Guided practice using the strategy with gradual release of responsibility:	
Teacher: *Now you read on silently. Every once in a while I will stop each of you and ask you where you have made predictions. We will talk about what evidence you are using to make your predictions and then read on to see if they comes true.*	As the teacher quietly checks in with each student, she continually draws attention back to the idea of how predictions help a reader better understand the book and make reading more interesting.

Example 6.1 (Continued)

	Students are taking responsibility for using the skill on their own, although the teacher is right there providing immediate and direct feedback.
Teacher moves from student to student and quietly checks in with each. Students' predictions are recorded on chart paper.	During the last 10 minutes of the lesson, the teacher guides students in a brief discussion about the predictions listed on the chart paper. The teacher also has one student share how one of his predictions had to be revised as more information was revealed.
5. Independent use of the strategy:	
Teacher: *We learned that we make predictions about ideas, characters, and what is important in a book. Now I would like you to go back to your seats and read this short poem about whales on your own. The directions I'd like you to follow are outlined on this sheet.* *1. Before you read, look it over and make some predictions about what you think the author is going to say about whales.* *2. While you are reading, pause after line four and make a prediction about what is going to come next and think about what evidence you are using to make your prediction. You might make some other predictions while you are reading.* *3. Work with your partner and quietly share one prediction you made before or during your reading and explain your thinking.* *4. In your writing journal, I'd like you to write about the prediction you shared with your partner and tell me how it helped you to better infer, or figure out, information the author wasn't directly saying in this poem. In your journal, you may also include any thoughts about other ways you infer every day. I have an example on this sheet for you to use if you get confused.* *Any questions? Nice job today!*	The teacher is confident that students will be successful as they work independently based on the information she gathered during the small group reading lesson. Explicit instruction in skills that support the strategy inferring will continue for several more weeks using several different types of text. Each subsequent lesson will give students many experiences in using the strategy across a variety of contexts. When students begin to gain more control over inferring and in understanding its role in the comprehension process, the amount of time spent on the first three steps of the lesson will be gradually shortened as the teacher releases more responsibility to the students, and the skills are increasingly integrated.

A second lesson example comes from a sixth grade classroom mid-year. The teacher is working in the back of the room with four students who need additional support in reading. The students have excellent decoding skills and "sound" like readers, but often do not comprehend what they have read. The teacher works with the students approximately 20 minutes, three times a week, while other students work independently. After four months, the teacher has already seen significant improvement in the students' reading comprehension.

Example 6.2 Small Group Reading Lesson

Strategy: Inferring.	Comprehension strategy emphasized during this lesson.
Focus Skill: Drawing conclusions.	The skill supporting the strategy inferring is the teaching point of this lesson.
Instructional Activity/Technique: Chart and discussion.	
Lesson Design:	The following five steps make up the lesson procedure.
1. Explicit description of the strategy—when the strategy should be used: Teacher: *Today we are continuing our work with the strategy inferring and the skill that supports this strategy, drawing conclusions. Remember we said drawing conclusions means a reader judges the relevant pieces of information presented by the author and comes to an interpretation that was not stated? We even drew a conclusion from the rhyme, "Itsy Bitsy Spider," after J. shared how his little sister loves to drive him crazy by singing the poem over and over!* Students laugh and nudge J. Teacher: *Does anyone remember the conclusion we drew from the information in that rhyme?* Student 3: *Something like if we don't succeed at first, we should keep trying.* Teacher: *Right! And that was never clearly stated by the author was it? Today we are going to talk more about how we as readers use information the author implies to help us draw conclusions.*	The teacher is building on previous learning using a different genre to further exemplify the teaching point.

(Continued)

Example 6.2 (Continued)

2. Teacher and/or student modeling of the strategy in action: Teacher: *We are going to be thinking about what readers do to draw conclusions using a chapter from the new book you will be discussing in your literature circles . . .* Walk Two Moons. *Before we work together, I am going to model how I am drawing conclusions to help support the inferring I need to do to fully appreciate and understand this book.* Teacher reads aloud title and first chapter. Teacher: *Now, I haven't read a lot of this story, but I can already start drawing conclusions from this first chapter. I am going to use the same chart we used with our previous book to think through my conclusions. First of all, when I go back to the first paragraph I notice the sentence, "My father plucked me up like a weed and took me and all our belongings . . . and we drove 300 miles straight north. . . ." I am going to write that in the first column* (writes sentence on the chart under the heading "Clues from the Author"). *Now, my background knowledge tells me that when people take all their belongings and drive far away they are leaving their home so I am going to write that in the second column on the chart under the heading "My Background Knowledge."* *I also noticed some negative words being used to describe the houses where they stopped . . . on the top of page 2, "The houses were all jammed together like a row of birdhouses . . . a tiny square of grass." And I also notice Sal is asking where things are in the next paragraph, "The barn? The river? The swimming hole?" I am going to write some of these key words in the first column.* (adds to chart) *I have found that when people describe things in a negative or sarcastic way they are not happy. I will write this idea in the second column.* (writes) *For example, I remember my son describing my car as a Match Box toy because he wanted us to have a bigger car.*	Teacher models the strategy by thinking aloud. The teacher is using a chapter from a text the students will soon be discussing with their peers in literature circles. She says she will not do this for every chapter of the book, but she plans to periodically use the literature circle text in her small group instruction. By doing so, she can provide explicit comprehension instruction and support the students' ability to fully participate in discussion of the content in their literature circle groups. Teacher is explaining her thinking and giving examples of the background knowledge she uses around each of the author's clues.

Teacher continues with a couple more examples from the text where the author implies information. Teacher: *So, I am beginning to look across at the information the author gave me and consider it with what my background knowledge is about similar things, and the conclusion I am drawing is that they moved and Sal is not happy about it. I'll write this in the third column under the heading, "Conclusion."*	
3. Collaborative use of the strategy in action: Teacher: *Are we ready to start Chapter 2 together?* *Let's all read page 4 and half of page 5 silently.* *I am noticing back in the first sentence something that might be important information. T., will you read that sentence out loud for the group?* Student 1 reads aloud. Teacher: *What might be important information there? What is the author not saying?* Student 2: *The adventures of Phoebe?* Teacher: *Tell us more about that and others help him out.* Student 4: *It sounds like a book title.* Teacher: *Yes! I think so too. So you are using your background knowledge to think about what the author might be trying to tell us in that first sentence. Let's start getting these ideas on the chart.* Teacher writes in first two columns. Teacher: *So, it was the adventures of Phoebe that led to Sal taking a trip to Idaho with her grandparents, although on page 5 we learn the real reasons for the trip were, "buried beneath piles of unsaid things." Are there clues in this list? Let's read them.*	Teacher is beginning to invite students to take more control over the lesson. The teacher initially directs the students' attention to a specific point in the text as they begin to practice drawing conclusions. The teacher's questions and prompts are leading the students to the work of figuring out what is being implied. The teacher restates and clarifies the ideas shared by the student to make sure everyone in the group is able to follow the thinking.

(Continued)

Example 6.2 (Continued)

Student 4: *Well, the author is using words like, "resting peacefully," "I wanted to see Momma, but I was afraid."*	
Student 3: *Yeah, it sounds like her mom's sick or something . . .*	
Teacher: *That's a conclusion you are beginning to draw. Let's put that over here in column 3 and I'll go back and add the words you just shared L., "resting peacefully, and so on" in the first column of our chart. (writes) Now what in your background knowledge made you think Sal's mom might be sick?*	The teacher accepts the student's response and then brings the focus back to explaining how the conclusion can be substantiated by implications in the text.
Student 3: *Cause let him rest in peace is what people say when someone is real sick but sleeping.*	
Teacher: *Good thinking. But the author didn't tell us that so you are drawing this conclusion from some of the information given but also with what you know.*	
Student nods.	
4. Guided practice using the strategy with gradual release of responsibility:	
Teacher: *Let's keep reading and see if we find any other clues and conclusions. Read to the top of page 7 and if you think the author is suggesting something important, put a small check in the margin with your pencil.*	Students are assuming responsibility for using the strategy on their own although the teacher is right there providing immediate and direct feedback.
Everyone checked a couple new important ideas the author is conveying. J., talk about why you put a check next to, "'I might as well catch a fish in the air."	Teacher carefully watches each reader and checks in individually as needed.
Student 4: *Because it is pretty impossible to catch a fish in air so I am thinking the author is saying Sal wants to do something almost impossible to do.*	
Teacher: *Does everyone see how J. used information from the text that didn't really state the meaning, and his background knowledge, to draw a conclusion about what the author is inferring?*	Teacher draws others' attention to the students' thinking.
Excellent job! And if you didn't do this as a good reader, you would not be making sense of Sal's story.	

5. Independent use of the strategy:	
Teacher: *What did you learn about drawing conclusions today?*	With time, the teacher will release more responsibility to the students, and help make sure they are integrating the other skills that support the strategy inferring as appropriate.
Student 1: *Authors don't always say everything straight out in their stories.*	
Teacher: *And?*	
Student 3: *You have to use the clues in the book and your background knowledge to draw conclusions.*	
Teacher: *Your thinking is right on target. To draw conclusions about what an author is implying, you need to use the information in the story and combine it with your background knowledge. Drawing conclusions helps readers infer and make sense of their reading.*	
I have a chart for you to use as you read the next chapter. Try doing the same thing that we did here together. Read and make a light check mark in your book when you think the author is dropping an important clue. Then extend that clue by using your background information. When you have a couple of examples, begin thinking about the conclusion you can draw. We won't always use a chart, but this will help you think about how this skill works.	The teacher has gathered enough information from the work in the small group to know that her students will be successful as they read the next chapter for homework.
Great! We'll pick up here tomorrow. Nice work today.	

Inferring is a key comprehension strategy for all recreational and academic reading. If a reader misses or misunderstands an author's implied meaning, comprehension begins to break down. As you can see by examining the skills that support the strategy inferring, there are many literary techniques that authors may use to suggest their points of view or purposes for writing. As students learn how to raise questions while reading, consider what they bring to the text, and make judgments about what the author is saying, they become better able to critique text, develop a critical stance, and understand at a deeper level.

INFERRING ACROSS CONTENT AREAS

This seventh grade social studies class is studying ancient river civilizations. The unit is organized around the conceptual lens "interactions." One of the focus questions students are investigating in this unit is, "How do artifacts reflect what we know about the culture of Ancient Egypt?" The teacher assigned each student a partner to find information that will help answer this question, and bring it back to the class ready to share the next day. As students set off in various directions (the library, the back table that was covered with a variety of resources, and to the computer stations in the back of the room), the teacher asked the two ELL students in the class if they would work with her in the back corner. They appeared relieved to have her support, and the lesson is described below.

Example 6.3   Small Group Sixth Grade Social Studies Lesson

Strategy: Inferring.	Comprehension strategy emphasized during this lesson.
Focus Skills: Synthesizing text clues and various types of connections.	The skill supporting the strategy inferring is the teaching point of this lesson.
Instructional Activity/Technique: Discussion.	
Lesson Design:	The following five steps make up the lesson procedure.
1. Explicit description of the strategy—when the strategy should be used:	
Teacher: *Let's reread the question we are trying to answer: How do artifacts reflect what we know about the culture of Ancient Egypt? Before we get started, do we understand what the question is asking? Let's see, I know we are beginning to understand what the word "culture" entails because we have talked a lot about this idea in previous lessons, but what about the word "artifacts?" Do you remember hearing that word before?*	The teacher checks on students' understanding of the task before starting the lesson.
Students look to the word wall in the front of the room.	
Student 1: (reads) *The objects, art, or items made by people.*	
Teacher: *Okay E., can you try to restate the question in your own words?*	Having the student restate the question in his own words helps plant an understanding more firmly in his mind before he begins.
Student 2: *How do things people make . . . show about their culture?*	
Teacher: *Excellent. So, today we want to figure out how objects that archaeologists found from ancient river valley civilizations tell us about the culture of the people who lived there, and since we are studying*	One of the greatest challenges is to find high quality content area text at appropriate reading levels for students. More publishers are trying to address

ancient Egypt as one example, let's see if we can find some information in this book to help us answer this question.	this issue, but teachers still spend considerable time locating resources. The book used in this lesson is published by National Geographic.
Now, authors don't always tell us every single idea they are thinking about as they write. Often readers need to do some work to figure out the information they may not be directly stating. This is called inferring. It is an important reading strategy because if we only read what is exactly stated in the book, we may miss some important information we were supposed to figure out. One way we infer is to put together or synthesize the clues or information the author is giving us so we get the full meaning.	Teacher offers the explicit explanation of the teaching point of this lesson.
When we synthesize text clues, we fill in details and information the writer is leaving out. The details we fill in are based on the background knowledge we bring to the text.	
In order for us to answer the question we are looking at today, I am going to pay close attention to the information and clues this author gives us about artifacts.	
Let me show you.	

2. Teacher and/or student modeling of the strategy in action:

Teacher: *Our book is* Egyptian Queens. *I'll read the introduction out loud.*	
Teacher reads aloud.	
Teacher: *I am going back to the first sentence. The author is telling me about a sculpture of the ancient Egyptian queen Nefertiti and gives a description of this sculpture. In the third sentence, the author talks about a stone carving of another queen, Hatshepsut. The author did not explicitly call these two items artifacts from Ancient Egypt, but from the definition we just talked about, I am sure they are. I am already thinking that this sculpture and stone carving could help us find information to answer our question because they sound like important artifacts. I am going to put a little post-it flag in the*	Teacher models the strategy by thinking aloud. Teacher reinforces the use of vocabulary that is still unfamiliar to the students.

Example 6.3 (Continued)

margin to go back to later because I know I am going to try to pull together all the clues at the end. Now I'm ready to keep reading. Teacher continues reading. Teacher: *I just found several more items that would be artifacts mentioned in this first paragraph: crafts, linen cloth, jewels, and pots. But, I am wondering how the author knows that many Egyptians had to work for the government each year. Were there artifacts that were found that told us that? I haven't read about any yet, so I will keep reading and look for clues.* Teacher continues reading. Teacher: *Now I am learning that the Egyptians invented a form of writing called hieroglyphics—in a complex and a simplified form—and their writing left behind more artifacts about the people. When I connect this information to what I was wondering about in the first paragraph I am able to fill in the details that the author did not state.*	 Teacher is careful to explain the reasons behind her thinking so that students will clearly follow her reasoning.
3. Collaborative use of the strategy in action: Teacher: *I am starting to pull some information together. Let's whisper read the top of page 5 together.* Teacher and students read. Teacher: *Did we find any information about artifacts in this section?* Student 1: *No things, but there is more information and we don't know where it comes from.* Teacher: *I like the way you are thinking about where the author would have learned this information. Let's read more and see if we can find and learn more about artifacts. We will whisper read together the first section.* Teacher and students read. Teacher: *Let's pause.* Student 2: *No artifacts are in this part either.*	 Teacher is beginning to invite students into the lesson. The teacher reinforces the student's thinking and also restates the word artifacts. Teacher clarifies the student's thinking.

Teacher: *Yes! I liked the way you used the vocabulary word, artifacts also. So, let's keep going.*	The teacher reinforces the student's use of the word artifacts.
Student 1: (stops reading) *It says we learned this from the writing on the walls of the temple.*	
Teacher: *Let's reread that part . . . so S., are you saying that that writing is the artifact that helped us learn about the information the author presented earlier?*	The teacher accepts the student's response and then brings the focus back to explaining how the conclusion can be substantiated by implications in the text.
Student 1: *Yes because otherwise how would we know?*	
Teacher: *That's exactly what I was thinking. Let's put a post-it note in the margin here, because this is important information that may help us figure out how this artifact helps us learn about the Egyptian culture.*	
Student 2: *And the picture shows the artifact.*	
Teacher: *The picture is definitely an artifact. Not the one S. was just talking about, the writing on the walls, but . . . tell me more about what you mean, E.?*	The teacher gives the student time to explain his response. Often the impulse is to jump in and respond for the struggling reader, but this teacher does a great job in letting students do the work and thinking.
Student 2: *It is the stone carving mentioned on the front page.*	
Teacher: (Turns back) *It is indeed. This looks like an important artifact that we need to learn more about. Do you see how you are putting information together to start figuring out more about the artifacts the author mentions? Keeping track of these clues is important so we can put them together at the end.*	
4. Guided practice using the strategy with gradual release of responsibility:	
Teacher: *Let's whisper read together the rest of this page. We'll stop at the end of each paragraph and you can tell me if you have found information or clues that we need to flag for the question we are trying to answer.*	The teacher whisper reads with the students in order to support them with the heavy vocabulary load of the text. The text includes the names of many Egyptian places and people, making the reading very challenging.
Teacher continues on in this manner for the rest of the chapter. Each time she pauses, she asks students the open-ended question, *Were there any clues in this paragraph?*	By keeping the prompt at the broadest level, students need to sift through the text and decide if there are any clues or not and how to make sense of the

Example 6.3 (Continued)

Teacher:	*Let's now look back at our post-it notes and see if we can put some of the information together to fill in gaps the author left and to help us respond to the question we are investigating. On the first page, we noted the information about a sculpture of Nefertiti and the stone carving of Hatshepsut. I'll write this down on this notepaper. Next, we flagged information about hieroglyphics because we felt this writing became an artifact that taught us a lot about the Egyptian culture. What was next?*
Student 1:	*The tools and the pyramids.*
Teacher:	*I'll include that . . . next?*

The teacher continues recording the information the students had marked with post-it notes in the text.

Teacher:	*Let's look over this information and put it together. Let's first focus on one artifact—the stone carving of Hatshepsut. From the information and clues the author gave us and from the connections you are making, can you tell us how this artifact reflects Egyptian culture?*
Student 1:	*This artifact shows how the people thought men kings were the most powerful because she wore men's clothes and had a beard and went fighting.*
Student 2:	*No, the fighting and the beard were from the artifact on the temple walls.*
Student 1:	*Oh yeah. . . . She just dressed like a king in the stone sculpture so she would be like a man king.*
Teacher:	*But let's go back to the important idea you mentioned about why she dressed like this.*
Student 1:	*Because men were always kings and queens were wives so if she was going to be king after her husband died, she thought she had to be more like a man.*
Student 2:	*Today queens can be like a king but still be queens, like in England.*
Teacher:	*So Queen Elizabeth doesn't have to dress like a man in order for people to respect her as a ruler?*
Student 2:	*Right.*

information. The teacher scaffolds her questions only if students begin to run into problems.

The teacher is starting to have the students synthesize the information. This can be overwhelming for readers when there is so much unfamiliar text vocabulary to work through.

Teacher: *And that is a great example of how a good reader puts together clues and information to really understand more than what the author is saying. We can see how this artifact might help us understand ancient Egyptian culture and how we would not see it today. Excellent thinking! Let's move on to one more artifact from the text.*	
5. Independent use of the strategy: Teacher: *You both did a great job synthesizing text clues and information that wasn't always in one place. You made connections and filled in gaps the author didn't spell out exactly for us. This was excellent inferring and we'll work on this some more as we go through the rest of the book.* *Now, so that you are prepared to share some information with the class tomorrow, I would like you to each think about all that we discussed with these two artifacts (points to sheet). For the next 15 minutes, I'd like you to find a quiet space in the room and rehearse your presentation. You did a great job and I know the class is going to enjoy hearing about these artifacts and what they tell us about Egyptian culture.*	The teacher is matching the learning from this lesson as closely as possible to the application expected tomorrow. She knows the oral rehearsal will help these students gain more confidence. The modeling and the inductive approach the teacher uses to help students work through their responses further supports their future success.

CONCLUSIONS AND REFLECTIONS

As readers read, they are constantly making inferences about the elements of text they need to "figure out" in order to reinforce and strengthen comprehension. There are many skills that underlie the strategy of inferring, and different types of text and purposes for reading demand utilizing these skills in different ways. A struggling reader needs to develop a metacognitive awareness of why and when to use the various skills that make up inferring in order to fully comprehend. Explicit instruction, extended time, and increased exposure to a variety of types of text that require students to grapple with inferring will assist in the development of a solid understanding of this essential comprehension strategy. If we want students to read and comprehend far more than the surface level of text, they must recognize that deep comprehension requires an engagement with text through a systematic use of strategies. Frequently, students who do not possess strong reading comprehension skills believe all the answers and information can be found word-for-word in the text. Consequently, inferring is one of the "Big Four" strategies worth teaching and worth teaching well.

Readers' Questions and Author's Answers

Q: My students use comprehension strategies when I am there to prompt them, but as soon as I leave them alone they stop using them. What do I do about this?

A: There may be several reasons why students' learning does not transfer. They may only have a surface level understanding of the strategy, the materials with which they are expected to use the strategies may be too quickly dissimilar from the text used in the original learning, the subsequent text may be too difficult, or the teaching prompts may be overly specific (can't generalize) and create a dependency. Reaching struggling readers is really hard work, which is why I encourage teaching partners to observe one another. Peer observations usually result in new insights that go unnoticed when we are so close to the situation.

The Gradual Release Lesson Design is critical to transfer also. The lesson design allows students to practice new learning with the teacher right there to guide and encourage them before expecting them to apply the strategies independently. Students with significant comprehension problems who are beyond the third grade have lots of years of experience with not reading well so our patience and persistence are important!

Q: In several sections of this book, there are references made to "the essential concepts of a discipline or lesson," and the term "conceptual lens" is used more than once. Can these terms be explained further?

A: Educational experts, such as Lynn Erickson (2007), show educators how to organize curriculum and deliver instruction to ensure students develop a deep understanding of complex ideas. Concepts are the mental constructs that frame the critical knowledge of a discipline. They are one or two word nouns that are timeless, universal, abstract (to different degrees), and broad. Examples of concepts in language arts include text structure, writer's craft, genre, and so on.

Concepts, Erickson explains, frame a set of examples that share common attributes. Since our brains organize new learning around concepts that we already know and understand, framing a lesson around a conceptual lens helps students use their background knowledge to unpack the new theme, issue, or problem being studied. Starting with a concept helps students better integrate new learning and look for patterns and connections across many different examples.

Erickson uses the conceptual lens (a selected concept) as a tool to help students process factual knowledge through to the conceptual level of thinking. This encourages the development of synergistic thinking between the factual and conceptual levels and engages a student's intellect at a deeper level, leading to meaningful understanding at both the factual and conceptual levels of knowledge.

We are now ready to move on to Chapter 7, which concludes our examination of the Four Powerful Strategies for struggling readers.

7

Conclusion

The test of literature is, I suppose, whether we ourselves live more intensely for the reading of it.

—Elizabeth Drew (1926)

This book is for all teachers who have struggling readers in their classrooms. The urgency to help readers who leave third grade with comprehension difficulties continually increases. As more learning expectations are inserted into a fixed number of school hours and days, the child whose reading comprehension is lagging, falls further and further behind. It is heartbreaking to imagine how lost a person with reading difficulties feels in today's fast-paced world.

Every day we are besieged by a barrage of information from which we cannot escape. The twenty-first century standards of literacy are directly affected by visual and electronic media becoming the more dominant forms of expression and communication. To participate fully in today's society and function competently in the workplace, it is essential to be capable of reading a broad range of texts quickly and well. Reading text well means that one must be able to move through an abundance of material with efficient comprehension. In many ways, information technologies make reading a more complex and rigorous process. They also make the ability to critically comprehend text more imperative so that the flood of irrelevant, biased, and superfluous information can be sorted out from the relevant, credible, and important.

Subject area curriculum units are typically designed with the assumption that students can read and keep up with the work. Struggling adolescent readers get caught in a double jeopardy as literacy standards increase and content area teachers have little time to address their literacy needs. When content area teachers organize lessons around concepts, or the big ideas that the facts exemplify, students begin to see the relevance of what is being taught, and they are better able to transfer their learning to other situations. When students comprehend their social studies, science, and business texts, they not only can think about reading strategies but also about the content they are learning.

Utilizing instructional techniques and activities that leverage literacy benefit all readers' comprehension. Also, using authentic literacy activities during strategy instruction can especially help support the at-risk readers' transfer of learning to new situations (see Chapter 1). Too often, the reading and writing tasks included in many publisher materials represent literacy activities that are contrived and can only be found in school (i.e., spelling lists, fill-in-the-blank worksheets, decodable text with questions at the end of each chapter, etc.). In these cases, students cannot find a similar purpose for the activity or type of text anywhere in their lives outside of school. This makes the transfer of literacy learning more difficult for struggling readers. Although some of these activities may help to demonstrate the strategy being taught, balancing them with more authentic assignments and tasks will better assist the at-risk reader who has a limited understanding of the comprehension process.

There is hope for the struggling adolescent reader and more people are beginning to pay attention. The Striving Readers Act (2007) proposes adolescent literacy grants be awarded to states according to poverty levels and eighth grade National Assessment of Educational Progress (NAEP) scores. Local districts will be able to use these funds to develop schoolwide literacy plans and provide professional development for teachers. To make progress, many students need continued reading instruction beyond the elementary grades (Ivey & Fisher, 2007, p. 71). Traditionally, however, the amount of guidance and support for reading instruction declines as students advance through the grades. As mentioned, this comes at a time when the expectations for successful and independent reading, along with the complexity of texts, are increasing. Fortunately, more people are beginning to pay attention and address the needs of these readers.

Effective teaching absolutely makes a difference! Teachers need opportunities to closely examine and discuss instructional practices in order to accelerate the struggling readers' progress. Understanding the comprehension process; using explicit, small group instruction in addition to whole class lessons; providing rich opportunities for students' interactions with meaningful and authentic literacy activities; teaching to concepts; and the gradual release of responsibility are some components that will make a difference in closing the gap between our proficient and struggling readers.

During the research and writing of this book, I had the joy of countless professional conversations with colleagues around the big ideas behind reading comprehension and effective instruction. We struggled to find common language that clearly defines strategies and skills, to determine what effective instruction looks like in practice, and how to deconstruct the complex process of comprehension without creating atomized, discrete parts that lose their connectivity to the bigger whole (strategy or concept). With shared terminology, our bantering began to reflect a greater level of specificity and our understanding deepened.

As dialogue continued, I noticed there was less concern invested in finding the origins of students' reading problems (looking in the rearview mirror) and more concern about *how* we could design effective interventions at the lesson level and across classrooms (looking forward). Discussions about instruction also began to shift from *the book* or the strategy itself to the *reader* and *how* proficient readers use strategies and skills as tools to construct meaning. We kept reminding each other that the purpose of comprehension instruction is to understand how strategies help students make sense of what they read and enable them to be more successful, independent readers. If instruction does not help students relate the teaching point of the lesson (strategy/skill) to the goal of comprehension, the transfer of learning is less likely to occur.

Working with struggling readers is challenging and rewarding work. Teachers who collaboratively design lessons, observe each other's practice, examine student work, and problem solve together, avoid the burnout that comes from working in isolation. Without a "critical friend" checking in once in a while, teaching and learning can easily stall. Frustration soon follows. The ideas and suggestions advocated in this book were put into practice by hundreds of teachers I worked with over the past ten years. We found that as knowledgeable colleagues observed each other's lessons, fresh insights to practices that helped nudge students to that next level were uncovered. We viewed and discussed video clips of lessons that not only gave confirmation of good teaching but offered powerful suggestions to better reach struggling readers. Everyone in our collaborative took responsibility for the success of every student rather than an individual teacher for just "his or her own."

The specific structure of the Gradual Release Lesson Design keeps student accountability high and students quickly realize that they—not the teacher—are expected to do the thinking! As teachers, we need to listen carefully when we ask students to explain their thinking and cite evidence for their responses. Initially, I find the common response of struggling readers to this request is, "I don't know," because there has seldom been an expectation that these students will know or because they are trying to read text that is too difficult to read. Students become capable of explaining their thinking once they deeply understand effective strategies, and when instruction utilizes text that is accessible to them. As lessons carefully link strategies and skills to previous learning, and are repeated across a variety of genres, students soon begin to notice how intertwined the strategies and skills used to construct meaning are. This is when you know students are really becoming active, metacognitive comprehenders.

Ludwig Mies van der Rohe (1886–1969) was one of the founding fathers of modern architecture. He is well known for his motto "less is more." As an architect, he sought a refined purity in architectural expression. Evident in Mies van der Rohe's magnificent skyscrapers (e.g., the Seagram Building in New York City), and his more modest accomplishments, is his goal of building economically in terms of sustainability—both in a technical and aesthetical way. An important principle he taught his students was that architects must completely understand their materials before they can design.

Like an expert architect, teachers must understand comprehension and the text that will be used to teach it before they can design interesting and effective lessons for students. The "Big Four" represent a "less is more" philosophy that promotes sustainable, clear, and in-depth strategy learning. The Four Powerful Comprehension Strategies are at the root of good reading. Deeply understanding the critical comprehension strategies discussed in Chapters 3–6, coupled with effective instruction from caring, committed teachers, will enable struggling readers to become successful and give them access to all that the rich world of print has to offer.

Writing this book has been a long, ever-changing, and richly rewarding learning experience. I always had great respect for the discipline of writing. This endeavor gave me an even higher regard for what it takes to close the space between an idea and its achievement. My own reading, reflection, and rereading of professional literature has been critical in this process, but equally important, as previously mentioned, was the great fortune I had to collaborate with many exceptional colleagues. The support and insights I gained from dialogue with other professionals cannot be understated. Their comments on the many drafts of this book significantly improved the end result. All educators need the opportunity to collaborate around ideas, experiences, student work, and professional reading because it ultimately transforms our understanding.

You might be wondering about how to move this book to practice.

Q: How do I start bringing the ideas advocated in this book to my classroom?

A: If you have a self-contained classroom, I would suggest starting by committing 20 to 30 minutes a day for small group instruction with your lowest-achieving group of readers. If you teach reading or another subject area and have multiple classes, I would suggest starting by identifying a target group of students in *one* class and building from there. The following outline might help you think about what you need to know and do to effectively begin implementing the ideas in this book.

1. **Do you know the approximate reading level of your target students?** If not, there are many assessment resources on the market such as the *Qualitative Reading Inventory-4* by Lauren Leslie and JoAnne Caldwell; *3-Minute Reading Assessments: Word Recognition, Fluency, and Comprehension, Grades 5–8*, by Timothy V. Rasinski, Nancy Padak, and Joanna Davis-Swing (Editors); and the *Developmental Reading Assessment 4–8*, by Joetta Beaver and Mark Carter.

   If these resources are not available, you can always hold a quick, one-on-one reading conference with your target students. Assemble texts with a range of readability levels, fiction and nonfiction, and ask students to orally read approximately one hundred words from a section. Note the number and type of miscues each student makes and the student's reading behaviors. If the student has difficulty reading ten or more of the one hundred words, the text is too difficult and you need to drop down a level and try again. This rough estimate will help you make appropriate text choices as you begin to pull together a collection of materials for your small group instruction.

2. **What text will you be using for small group instruction?** If you use a reading anthology, be cautious. The readability of anthologies bounces considerably from one selection to the next. If struggling readers are trying to plow through reading that is too difficult, they will not have the stamina to reflect on the reading strategies you are working so hard to teach, so you may need to be selective about which parts of an anthology you use.

   If you are fortunate to have available a range of texts at various reading levels and genres, it is important you take the time to read them. It is better to delay using a longer, unfamiliar book and use short nonfiction articles, fables, short stories, or selected chapters until you have a chance to read the books. This is where a knowledgeable public librarian or a school library-media teacher is invaluable.

   Text selection takes time and is a balancing act. You want to start with simpler, shorter texts (across a range of genres) that help exemplify the Four Powerful Strategies. Sometimes teachers use different chapters of a selection for strategy instruction. The caution here is that students need practice in a variety of genres to promote deep understanding of the strategy. If the book is too long, the opportunities to vary genre become limited.

   You also want a collection of texts that gradually build in complexity and readability so that as students become more proficient in their strategy use, they practice in gradually more difficult texts. Again, this task will not feel so daunting if undertaken with colleagues. I know grade level teams of teachers who have made sorting and categorizing texts their annual performance goal and accomplished wonders in a year's time.

3. **How do I schedule my small group reading instruction?** Because each school situation is different, there is not a one-size-fits-all answer to this. I do notice that teachers who truly make the commitment find the time. It may be helpful to think of instruction on a continuum. The more frequent the instruction and the closer it is to students, the greater the acceleration of learning will be. So, as we think about struggling readers who desperately need to accelerate their ability to read well, we need to try our best to meet with them in a small group for 20 to 30 minutes (no longer!) every day. If additional support is available for these students (pull-in or pull-out) it should not take the place of the teacher's daily, small group work with them. Rather, it should be another opportunity for them to practice the same lessons the teacher is providing. When content area teachers also support literacy, the results can be even more powerful.

4. **How can I integrate the Four Powerful Strategies with my commercial reading program that preteaches strategies in whole group and then reteaches them in small groups?** I find the lesson objective of many commercial reading programs varies from one day to the next and from being a strategy or a skill. Many typical and advanced readers can handle the bouncing around; however, struggling readers try to survive the day then start over with the next lesson. These are the

students who have difficulty transferring and integrating their learning across lessons, which is why their progress is never enough from year to year in programs like this.

Many of the new commercial programs do have texts at lower readability levels (intervention books) available for small group instruction, but again, often the teaching points are disconnected and not sustained over time. My suggestion is to start by moving away from the teacher's manual during small group instruction of fragile readers. Create lesson plans for these students using the Four Powerful Comprehension Strategies with the Gradual Release Lesson Design. Even if you use the intervention texts that are part of the commercial program, your students will be better served by the explicit, stable, focused instruction you will be providing.

5. **How should lessons map across the school year?** First, the long-term goal is for struggling readers to become capable readers who can transfer the skills and strategies necessary to independently read with deep understanding. This book is devoted to discussing effective instruction for students who are in third to eighth grade and are still confused about how to comprehend text. So, in the beginning, ensuring students are able to independently practice the teaching point (a skill connected to a specific strategy) of each lesson is the daily goal. Interim goals are to slowly increase the readability of the text, vary the genre, increase the complexity of the literacy tasks students are practicing, move the teaching point of lessons from one skill to the integration of skills that support the focus strategy, and then to the integration of multiple strategies.

The Gradual Release Lesson Design needs to be considered across the year also. As was explained in earlier chapters, when a new skill or strategy is introduced, the first two steps of the lesson may require more time. As students become more capable, the first two steps become shorter and more time is spent with collaboration and guided practice. As the year progresses, the time spent on the first three steps is reduced and guided practice takes up at least two-thirds of the lesson.

As teachers see students gaining more success with comprehension, there is a greater release of explicit instruction and greater increase of the integration of strategies. All of this requires instruction that closely follows the students. As teachers, we need to understand our struggling readers' strengths and weakness while planning how we can move them forward. The goals are targets to always be moving toward, but the progress the students are making becomes the real road map.

Glossary

Defining Terms: Are We Speaking the Same Language?

Words that carry specialized meanings in one community can be interpreted differently by another, particularly where individuals in the second community have little access to the dialogues in the first. . . .

—Heather C. Hill (2001)

This is a book of ideas for teaching reading comprehension. It is primarily directed toward teaching struggling readers, although the concepts and suggestions presented may benefit all students who are learning to read for deep understanding. It is important that you, the reader, and I, as writer, have common definitions of specific terms used throughout this book. By *fixing* our language—establishing the limits of some essential terms in this publication— I hope to deepen readers' understanding of the ideas presented.

In reviewing professional literature and research, and in listening to various experts in the field, it quickly becomes apparent how easy it is to be confused with terminology. Frequently, you will find terms such as strategies, skills, and processes used interchangeably in reading comprehension literature. Depending on which author is being read, the list of most effective reading strategies grows longer or shorter. Sometimes it is difficult to distinguish whether a recommended strategy is intended to describe a teacher's means of instruction or to describe a reader's reading behavior. Even though different authors may use the same term, there can be shades of difference in the meaning they attach to it.

Your understanding of the terms used throughout this book will significantly deepen your understanding of the ideas presented. Therefore, this Glossary is important, and I hope you have turned to it early in your reading.

In any discussion of the reading process, "fuzziness" persists no matter who attempts to separate and precisely define terms. Pearson and Johnson (1978) acknowledge unclear and overlapping terminology is actually due to the strong interface between reading processes. So, while reading this Glossary, please remember that although I attempt to classify terms to communicate a distinction among the ideas under discussion, the list is really an arbitrary convenience—the terms and definitions are not totally distinct and absolute, because the strategies and skills share many common characteristics. With this said, let's now look at some of the key terms used in this text. The terms are not alphabetized but rather listed in the order explained in this book.

Reading Strategies: Sinatra, Brown, and Reynolds (2002) define strategies as goal-directed, cognitive operations over and above the processes that are a natural consequence of carrying out a task. In other words, strategies take more conscious thought and are utilized to address a specific reading goal. Strategies are complex because many reading skills are situated within a reading strategy. *In order to effectively employ a strategy, the reader must have control over a variety of the skills that support the strategy, be fluent and flexible in the utilization of these skills, and appropriately integrate the other relevant skills and strategies.* A strategy may be thought of as a systematic plan readers consciously adapt and monitor to improve their learning performance (Harris & Hodges, 1995). Strategies are active comprehension processes that a reader chooses in order to comprehend well (Irwin, 1989).

If we want students to comprehend with greater depth, we as educators need to set priorities amid the myriad of reading competencies listed in state standards, local curriculum, basal readers, and professional journals. As mentioned previously, various authors are beginning to attempt to identify the "big" strategies independent readers use to comprehend text (Allington, 2001; Duke & Pearson, 2002; Keene & Zimmermann, 1997; Pearson, Roehler, Dole, & Duffy, 1992). This book recognizes four comprehension strategies that are worth spending time teaching and that are essential for understanding text. These strategies are

- **summarizing**
- **creating meaningful connections**
- **self-regulating**
- **inferring**

Details of each these Four Powerful Strategies are included in Chapter 3–6, along with sample lessons showing teachers in action. Each of the four strategies and the skills that support them are defined in this Glossary.

Reading Skills: Skills are the smaller operations or actions that are embedded in strategies and, when appropriately applied, they "allow" the strategies to deepen comprehension. That is to say, if a reader has control over the skills that underpin a strategy, more energy is available for utilizing the strategies necessary for deeper comprehension.

Reading skills refers to the parts of acts (strategies) that are primarily intellectual (Harris & Hodges, 1995). This text identifies numerous skills that fortify the Four Powerful Comprehension Strategies. For example the strategy *inferring* is supported by such skills as using background knowledge, questioning, determining theme, determining author's purpose, making predictions, and drawing conclusions. A strategic reader uses many of these skills in concert as he or she makes sense of text. For example, in reading Chapter 9 of *Lord of the Flies*,

"A View to a Death," I might begin by using the skill questioning as I ask myself, "Is a character going to die? What clues will the author give me as to who it might be or how it might happen? How will a death change the relationships of the characters?"

Do you see how the skill of questioning (and others) helps me focus on and plan for the strategy inferring, which I need to use in order to understand my reading of this chapter?

Instructional Activities/Techniques: The means that teachers use to ensure students become capable, confident comprehenders of text. Many authors refer to the terms "instructional strategies" and "instructional activities" interchangeably. As defined above, *strategies* represent goal-directed cognitive operations. I want to make a clear distinction between the term "reading strategies" (what the *reader* is doing) and the term "instructional strategies" (what the *teacher* is doing or facilitating during strategy instruction). Thus, teachers use various instructional *activities* or *techniques* to leverage their strategy instruction. Some familiar instructional activities teachers use include completing graphic organizers, marking the text with post-it notes, whole group discussion, think-pair-share, and so on. These activities are all commonly used as a means of support for clarifying the teaching point of a lesson, for enabling the teacher to check student understanding, and for helping students be mindful of their literacy processes.

Gradual Release Lesson Design: The teacher's role in teaching students to effectively apply reading strategies is to maximize the likelihood that students will transfer their learning to new contexts independently. The five-step lesson procedure or lesson design advocated in this book is designed to scaffold the effective teaching of strategies in order to maximize transfer of students' learning. These steps are well researched (Duke & Pearson, 2002) and are used as a template for each small group reading lesson (see Figure G.1). The steps are:

1. An explicit description of the strategy and how, when, where, and why to use it

2. Teacher and/or student modeling of the strategy in action

3. Collaborative use of the strategy in action

4. Guided practice using the strategy with gradual release of responsibility

5. Independent use of the strategy

Through these teaching procedures, the transfer of learning to other situations will be enhanced to a much greater degree—especially for struggling readers (Wood, 1998). Using all the steps of this lesson design balances explicit instruction with opportunities for students to read, write, and discuss texts, and it connects and integrates these different learning opportunities. Chapter 2 is devoted to explaining the lesson procedure in greater detail. The steps of the lesson are used consistently yet flexibly so they follow the reader's responses. The amount of time spent on each step will begin to shift as more or less scaffolding is necessary.

Figure G.1 Teaching for Strategies

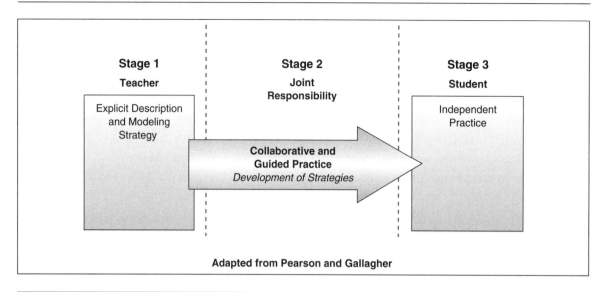

Adapted from Pearson and Gallagher

SOURCE: This figure was adapted from the figure published in *Contemporary Educational Psychology*, Volume 8, Issue 3, P. David Pearson and Margaret C. Gallagher, "The Instruction of Reading Comprehension," Page 337, Academic Press (1983).

Finally, as with any good instruction, comprehension instruction needs to be accompanied by ongoing assessment. Teachers should carefully monitor students' use of comprehension strategies and skills in each phase of the lesson and adjust the lesson according to student responses.

Transfer: The transfer of students' learning is universally accepted as the ultimate aim of teaching (McKeough, Lupart, & Marini, 1995). Broadly defined, transfer refers to the degree to which prior learning affects new learning or performance. A rich repertoire of teaching practices is necessary to facilitate transfer. That is, instruction needs to include extensive modeling, explaining, scaffolding, and coaching with students taking increasing responsibility for the independent use of strategies over time (El-Dinary, 2002). The manner in which new learning occurs affects subsequent transfer. Information that is presented in the context of solving problems, for example, is more likely to be spontaneously used than information presented in the form of simple facts. Transfer requires a sufficient degree of original learning and an understanding of the strategy—the features of the strategy, why it is important, and how and when it can be best utilized. Without this differentiated knowledge of performance requirements, students may apply their knowledge in the wrong settings or may not be able to assess their performance (Bransford & Swartz, 1999).

To strengthen transfer, comprehension strategies and skills need to be presented in multiple instructional contexts and through "what if" problem solving. Additionally, instruction needs to require children to invent solutions that can be generalized to a broad class of problems rather than simply to attempt to solve a single problem (Bransford & Swartz, 1999).

Text: The term text is used to describe any language event—oral, written, or visual—in any format.

DEFINING THE FOUR POWERFUL COMPREHENSION STRATEGIES AND SUPPORTING SKILLS

The following definitions of the "Big Four" Strategies and supporting skills are drawn from a wide span of resources, conversations, and experiences. The goal of defining these terms is to create a common vocabulary between reader and writer and to make explicit the reciprocity these strategies and skills have with one another. You will find there is overlap across some of the terms. For example, you will notice some of the skills listed under one strategy are at work in the other strategies. This is all due to the highly interactive nature of the comprehension process. This is why the benefits of learning even one strategy transcend across others and result in improved comprehension for struggling readers.

As you continue to think deeply about the most effective comprehension strategies and skills, you may find skills to add or delete or reword. The list below has been revised many times and continues to be a work in progress as more colleagues provide feedback and discussion about how important language is in communicating comprehension to students.

Summarizing: Summarizing is an analytical process. This strategy involves representing, in a few sentences and in your own words, the most important ideas of a longer passage or selection. It is a mixture of reducing a long text to a short text by selecting relevant information. The final steps in any critical reading are distilling and summarizing information. A good summary shows how well the text is understood.

Skills that support the strategy *summarizing* are discussed below.

- **Identifying important information (main idea):** This skill requires one to distinguish the core concepts in a selection (that will be included in the summary) from the supporting or minor information (that will not be included in the summary). Deleting unnecessary and redundant information to reduce material to the main ideas requires close reading. The important information becomes apparent as the reader filters out the supporting details and the ideas that may be repeated information.
- **Distinguishing between a topic and a main idea:** A topic is the general subject dealt with in a text or discussion. A main idea is the important thought (implied or expressed) that the author is conveying about the topic. For example, in an article on alternative fuel (topic), the author may be making a case that the focus on alternative fuel sources is harming other important industries (main idea). The ability to distinguish between the topic and the main idea is a foundational skill in effectively summarizing.
- **Generalizing important information and ideas (concepts):** A generalization is a broad statement that describes the relationship of two or more concepts (or main ideas). Generalizations reflect deeper, conceptual understanding, and they hold true across other situations. Generalizing important information and ideas requires a reader to grasp

the gist of a text's message without becoming preoccupied with the facts, examples, and details that the author includes as evidence to support a position or idea. A generalization is formed by thinking across the ideas presented, and determining what they have in common.

A generalization is a specific kind of conclusion. All generalizations are conclusions, but not all conclusions are generalizations; there is a distinct difference. For example, after reading a book about butterflies, one *conclusion* a reader may draw is, "Butterflies are very fragile creatures."

Although the author never directly states butterflies are fragile, the reader draws this conclusion by using information in the story along with what she already knows. She supports her conclusion by citing the descriptions of the changes a butterfly goes through and by discussing how vulnerable the butterfly is to weather and foe in each stage.

After reading the same book, a reader may form some *generalizations* such as, "Changes in a life cycle can be observed and measured." This statement describes the relationship of several ideas (concepts) that were discussed in the book (changes, life cycle, observation, and measurement), reflects the reader's understanding of these ideas, and also holds true across other situations (the life cycle of other animals, plants, etc.).

This skill (identifying and generalizing important information) aids summarizing because it requires a reader to analyze and differentiate relevant and irrelevant information. It also requires that the reader [listener] be aware of the devices that authors use as signals when stressing the importance of ideas (e.g., introductory statements, topic sentences, summary sentences, italics, underlining, repetition, etc.).

- **Determining and sequencing events and ideas:** Constructing summaries requires readers to track, order, and restate events described in the material being read. An event is an occurrence, especially one that is particularly significant, interesting, exciting, or unusual.

  Authors may use clue words such as first, then, finally, last, while, during, and after to help alert readers to a new event. A change in a character's action or an introduction of a character may also signal the next occurrence. In summarizing, the important incidents (events) in text are presented in the same sequence as in the original text.

- **Identifying genre:** Genres are categories or classifications of text formed by sets of conventions. Some selections may cross into multiple genres by way of borrowing and recombining these conventions. As a reader learns to recognize genre, organizational patterns of the genre become more recognizable. For example, after identifying text genre (such as fantasy, science fiction, realistic or historical fiction, informational text, etc.), the reader can begin to expect certain vocabulary, punctuation, writing style, text features (headings, subheadings), and literary devices (rhyme, bias, foreshadowing) appropriate to the genre. This awareness guides summarizing and supports comprehension.

- **Identifying type of text structure:** How is the information organized? Authors make decisions about how to present information to readers depending on the type of text. Some structures are more representative of specific genres (fiction and nonfiction) and may use specific features (bold headings) to support the text structure. Common text structures include:

  o *Chronological/Sequence:* (Time/Order) Chronological articles and books unveil events in a sequence from beginning to end. Words that signal chronological structures include: first, then, next, finally, and specific dates and times. Biographies are often written using a chronological text structure.

  o *Cause/Effect:* Informational texts often describe cause and effect relationships. The text describes events and identifies or implies causal factors.

  o *Problem/Solution:* The text introduces, creates, and describes a problem and presents solutions.

  o *Compare/Contrast:* Authors use comparisons to describe ideas to readers. Similes, metaphors, and analogies are frequently used in compare/contrast organizational structures.

  o *Descriptive:* Sensory details help readers visualize and connect to information.

  o *Classical:* This text structure conforms to specific genre but usually begins with a harmonious introduction, followed by a problem or conflict that disturbs the harmony; a hero may emerge in the quest to regain harmony, and finally the happy ending.

  Identifying text structure helps a reader read more efficiently and helps organize ideas for synthesizing and summarizing. Students should learn how to preview text prior to reading to gain a sense of the type of text and its structure(s). Summarizing is easier when one has a clear sense of structure for organizing the material. A summary should follow the same structure as that in the original text.

  Note: All of the Four Powerful Comprehension Strategies benefit from an understanding of text structures.

- **Categorizing and classifying using text information and background knowledge:** This skill requires one to sort and organize information (especially in longer selections). Categorizing is grouping the facts and ideas from the selection; classifying is then taking note of the similar and/or distinct attributes of the ideas or examples presented. This skill helps readers see how ideas are related and helps distinguish the essential from the nonessential resulting in a more cohesive summary.

- **Paraphrasing:** Paraphrasing is restating or explaining ideas in your own words while retaining the meaning and ideas in the original selection. It is a legitimate way (when accompanied by accurate documentation) to borrow from a source. It is a valuable skill because the mental process required for successful paraphrasing helps a reader grasp the full meaning of the original text. Paraphrasing also helps young readers check their own comprehension. In summarizing, the tendency of young and struggling readers is to restate the original text. Therefore, paraphrasing is a necessary skill in learning about the strategy summarizing.

- **Questioning:** Questions that support the strategy summarizing include: *After scanning the text, which text structure did the author use to organize the information? How does this paragraph relate to the text information read so far? How did the author organize the text to be "reader-friendly?" Which text features helped me collect information from the article? What are the essential points the author is making? How might I use the events described in the text to create a timeline of events? How can the information from this selection be presented visually? Which graphic organizer would I use to present the information in this selection?*

- **Synthesizing concepts and events:** Synthesizing is putting parts (ideas) together into a unified whole. A well-developed summary includes statements of new insights acquired as a result of synthesizing the ideas presented in a piece. Readers first determine the key ideas and then incorporate this new information into their existing knowledge base. Integrating information in this manner creates an insightful understanding of the text and extends a literal summary to an inferential level of meaning.

Creating Meaningful Connections: The significance of the strategy creating meaningful connections lies within the transaction between reader and text—text language may suggest a connection that is entertainment for one person but may be unexpectedly emotional for another. It is important to remember that in teaching this strategy, students learn to create *meaningful* connections—connections that deepen their understanding of what is being read. In contrast, surface level connections do not result in significantly increasing comprehension.

Skills that support the strategy *creating meaningful connections* are discussed below.

- **Imaging:** This skill is the process of forming sensory images (visual, tactile, auditory, etc.) while reading or listening. Gambrell and Koskinen (2002) describe imaging as a form of active processing that helps students acquire a more meaningful representation of text. An image may be based on experience or imagination. It is evoked by a reader (or listener) connecting or reacting to the author's descriptive details.

- **Being aware of text language:** Authors use sensory language and other writers' craft techniques to help readers visualize ideas and make connections. Authors recognize that people store a vast bank of impressions in their sensory memory from their life experiences as well as their knowledge of other text and the world. Noticing the way an author deliberately or subtly uses word play, descriptions, metaphors, references, and so on to rouse a reader's heart, mind, and memory supports the strategy creating meaningful connections.

- **Activating prior knowledge/experience:** Schema is the background knowledge/information and experience readers activate and bring to the text. Schema theory explains how these prior experiences, knowledge, emotions, and understandings affect what and how people learn. Proficient readers actively use their background knowledge and experience to construct images and make connections with text. Doing so helps them make sense of what they are reading. Struggling readers often do not consider whether the text makes sense based on their own background knowledge, or whether their knowledge can be used to help them understand confusing or challenging material. Additionally, struggling readers often just do not have the life experiences that others have that enable them to create connections. We therefore need to know our students and make relevant text selections for them.

  Accessing prior knowledge and experiences is a good starting place when teaching reading strategies because students have experiences, knowledge, opinions, and emotions that they can draw upon. Harvey and Goudvis (2000) discuss all of the above but also caution that merely making connections is not the goal. Connections that do not contribute to a better understanding of text can actually be a distraction. Readers need to analyze how their connections are contributing to their comprehension of text.

- **Previewing:** Linda Dorn and Carla Soffos (2005) tell us some of the skills of previewing text are accomplished in a short amount of time. A reader looks over (1) the back cover and inside flap, (2) excerpts of reviews and information on awards the book may have won, (3) the first page or lead paragraph, and (4) the table of contents. Previewing skills cause the reader to think about what he or she knows about the author, the topic, or the genre prior to approaching the reading task. Reading the title, flipping through the pages to check out the features of the book such as the general layout, the length, the illustrations, graphics, headings, and perhaps the writing style all help the reader to begin formulating predictions about the text.

  Previewing is central to how well a reader will interact with the text as previewing develops the reader's purpose for reading and activates the mind for creating connections. Readers who lack the ability to preview texts for meaningful connections are likely to have impaired comprehension (Dorn & Soffos, 2005). Teaching previewing skills also helps students become more competent in self-selecting text that is appropriate to their reading level; this is another important behavior of an independent reader.

- **Making text connections:** Keene and Zimmermann (1997) tell us readers comprehend better when they activate different kinds of connections (listed below). Connections are derived from one's background information/experiences but most important, good readers expand upon their connections and can describe how they used the connection to deepen their understanding of text.

   o **Text-to-self** are highly personal connections that a reader makes between a piece of reading material and one's own life experiences. For example, "I know how the character must feel because I miss my dad too."

   o **Text-to-text** connections remind readers of other materials that they have previously read. This may include selections by the same author, stories from the same genre, or perhaps articles on the same topic. Thinking about how the new text connects to other familiar works, ideas, or information supports critical reading and deeper understanding. For example, "This text structure in this new book is the same as the one used in the author's previous book that I read last year. Recognizing this helped me know what to expect."

   o **Text-to-world** connections are the larger, vicarious connections that a reader brings to a reading situation. The things we learn through the Internet, movies, magazines, television, and newspapers create a sense of how the world works that takes us beyond our personal experiences. For example, "I heard a television commentator discuss the topic in this article and I am thinking about how that information compares to what I am reading."

- **Questioning:** The skill of questioning to support the creating meaningful connections strategy requires readers to question how text information fits with their background information and experiences. Doing so extends comprehension beyond the surface level, helps readers broaden their knowledge, and keeps readers engaged with text. Question examples include:

  Text-to-self: *What does this remind me of in my life? Has something like this ever happened to me? How is this similar/different from my experiences?*

  Text-to-text: *What parts remind me of another book I've read? How is this information the same or different from other things I have read? Have I read about something like this before? Where in this book did the author give other hints about the character's motives?*

  Text-to-world: *What does this remind me of in the real world? How is this similar to or different from things that happen in the real world?*

- **Synthesizing various types of connections and text:** This skill calls for putting together and making sense of information from texts and one's own connections with text (text-to-self, text-to-text, text-to-world) to create new meaning. In using this skill one must have the ability to recall background information, infer relationships among sources, and draw a conclusion based on sound reasoning. The end result may be a new perspective, focus, idea, or an awareness of misconceptions, any of which strengthen comprehension. Synthesizing knits together and makes sense of the meaningful connections good readers make.

Self-Regulating: This strategy requires an active awareness and knowledge of one's mental processes (metacognition) and knowing what to do in order to accomplish the goal of comprehension. Self-regulating is a reader's recognition of the successes and failures in creating meaning from text, and adjusting one's reading processes accordingly. The two basic processes occurring simultaneously (*monitoring your progress* as you learn and *making changes and adapting* your strategies if you perceive you are not doing well) make the strategy of self-regulating a critical underpinning of reading comprehension. As readers become proficient with using self-regulating skills, they gain confidence and become more independent as learners.

Skills that support the strategy *self-regulating* are discussed below.

- **Knowing self as a learner, knowing the reading task, and knowing the reading strategies/skills:** If there is a conscious awareness of what we know about ourselves as learners, we are on our way to learning how to self-regulate. This requires knowing our strengths and weaknesses so that a proactive plan can be developed that will support our success. The plan may include articulating a reading goal to help keep us focused and on the right path, surrounding ourselves with the resources we feel we may need to complete the task, finding the right space, and estimating the time we may need. These actions are all elements of knowing ourselves as learners.

  Knowing the reading task is another important aspect of this skill. Too often, a struggling reader jumps into reading without thinking about what the task is really about. To reduce anxiety and enable the focus to be on comprehension, readers can clarify the expectations of the task, identify how performance will be evaluated, and think through the support materials that may be needed.

  Finally, a reader needs to know what the strategy self-regulating entails. An oral or mental rehearsal of the reading strategies and skills that will help keep track of comprehension increases the probability that they will be applied. Having the awareness that meaning has broken down and then knowing how to effectively use reading strategies and skills to get back on track is crucial. Readers learn to monitor their own learning and meaning through reflection and feedback (from self and others). Keeping a log of one's progress is a way to encourage self-reflection and motivation to improve.

- **Knowing the purpose for reading:** Ron Fry (1994) suggests that there are six fundamental purposes for reading:

  1. To grasp a certain message

  2. To find important details

  3. To answer a specific question

  4. To evaluate what you are reading

  5. To apply what you are reading

  6. To be entertained

Knowing the purpose for reading determines the goals a reader seeks to accomplish while reading. The skill of knowing the purpose for reading directs which monitoring skills need to be used and the reading rate. It is an important aspect of self-regulating.

- **Looking back, rereading, and reading ahead:** Most struggling readers believe that something must be wrong with them if they must read a textbook chapter or article more than once or look back over text features they previously skimmed. Good readers, especially when reading less familiar topics, recognize when reading material once is not enough. Looking back at charts, graphs, illustrations, captions, names, punctuation patterns, and other information helps readers organize, clarify, and recall information.

  Rereading builds fluency and is a skill used frequently in self-regulating. Rereading and looking ahead are also effective skills used to help sort out unknown words and other confusions. However, this is not to imply that tenacious rereading will automatically result in improved self-regulating. Rereading needs to be for a specific purpose (to sort out where meaning broke down or to gain a deeper understanding). This may mean rereading a sentence or looking back at a previous page for clarification. A general sense of understanding might be gained in the first reading; second round reading may raise an awareness and appreciation of previously unnoticed details, text language, punctuation, or text features.

  If an unknown word is causing confusion, the definition may emerge by reading ahead. When meaning is interrupted, good readers do not perceive themselves as failures; instead, they reanalyze the task to achieve better understanding. The strategy self-regulating consistently incorporates the skills looking back, rereading, and reading ahead.

- **Predicting, confirming, clarifying, and revising:** Making predictions means describing what you think will be revealed next in the selection based on clues from the title, illustrations, and text details. Predictions before reading are based on previewing or skimming text and asking questions. Examining text details during reading provides clues to make predictions. Readers confirm, clarify, or revise their predictions during and after reading based on knowledge of text structure, characters, previous knowledge of the author or genre, and other sources of information. By verifying and refining predictions, a reader is checking the validity of his or her thinking based on information collected from a text. Predicting sets expectations for reading, which makes reading more meaningful and easier to remember.

- **Problem solving words, phrases, or paragraphs:** Problem solving skills may take many forms. Using the meaning of prefixes, suffixes, and word roots may help unlock an unknown word. Proficient readers also use information from text (context) to decipher unfamiliar words. Context refers to the words that come before and/or after an unfamiliar word or phrase.

  Textbooks may restate an unfamiliar word using common synonyms or examples. These techniques help readers make associations (if a direct definition is not provided) to challenging vocabulary. Sometimes an author's descriptive details enable a reader to get the gist of the text.

  Readers need to know a variety of problem solving skills in order to self-regulate their comprehension. When problems cannot be resolved independently, seeking assistance from other resources is needed.

- **Cross-checking multiple sources of information:** This self-regulating skill requires bringing together at lease three sources of text information simultaneously. (e.g., A reader must ask: "Does this *make sense* with what is happening in the text, and with my background knowledge? Am I reading words that represent correct *syntax* and book language? Does what I am reading match the *letter-sounds* on the page?") Decoding by checking meaning against letter-sounds and syntax is an early reading skill but also applies to older readers who encounter new and challenging vocabulary. Other information sources (illustrations, charts, background knowledge, etc.) can also be used to confirm meaning.

- **Adjusting reading rate:** The skill of knowing when and how to skim and scan for specific information and when to read more slowly is closely tied to the purpose for reading. Intimate, slower reading is often necessary when a subject is unfamiliar. If one's reading rate is too measured, however, fluency and comprehension can be negatively affected. The skill of learning to adjust one's reading rate according to the purpose and the complexity of the material is essential to the strategy self-regulating. Consciously forcing oneself to read faster can improve reading rate, but reading quickly should never be at the expense of reading comprehension. Concentrating on the purpose for reading (e.g., locating main ideas and details, and really focusing on finding them quickly) is the best way to improve both reading rate and comprehension.

- **Questioning:** Questions (asked of oneself) that support self-regulating include: *What is going on in this text? Why am I reading this? Are there words I don't understand? Is there information that doesn't agree with what I know? How has the author tried to help me understand the vocabulary? Based on the title, what information do I expect to read in this selection? Based on the information I have read so far, what do I predict will come next? What do I need to help me understand this type of text?*

- **Synthesizing text with background information:** This skill is an ongoing part of the strategy self-regulating. Meaning is being constructed and adjusted constantly as a reader analyzes text information against the background information he or she brings to the text. An interpretation, a theory, and an understanding of "the big picture" begin to emerge from all the separate pieces of information.

Inferring: This strategy involves seeing and considering ideas that are not literally on the printed page. Inferring can be a complex strategy for struggling readers. To figure out meaning that may be intended or implied rather than directly stated by an author, a reader must combine a number of pieces of information from text. It requires thinking about what may be only suggested or hinted at in a selection. Sometimes the most important message in a piece of text is on an inferential level.

If you infer that something has happened, you do not see, hear, feel, smell, or taste the actual event, but using the information and your background knowledge, you make sense of the event. We make inferences every day—most of the time without thinking about it. Helping struggling readers bring this realization to text will help them learn the skills of inferring.

Skills that support the strategy *inferring* are discussed below.

- **Using background knowledge:** The importance of the background knowledge a reader brings to text became recognized in what is known as schema theory. Reading is now understood to be an active process of constructing meaning by connecting one's own knowledge and prior experiences with the information found in text. If readers have minimal or no background knowledge about the topic being read, they will miss authors' inferences, find the reading challenging, and be unable to use the other essential skills of this strategy. For this reason, prior to using a text, it is imperative to determine whether or not students have the key background knowledge they will need.

- **Determining author's purpose:** Determining an author's purpose is identifying the reason or reasons an author wrote a selection. Readers must ask, "Why do you think the author wrote the article?" Authors may have more than one purpose for writing. Often a reader has to infer an author's intent. Inferring the author's intention for writing (or speaking) helps a reader figure out other subtle messages that might be in the text. For example, if the purpose is to persuade, the reader needs to carefully scrutinize the evidence and reasons behind the author's argument and determine if they are valid. The strategy inferring is strengthened by the skill of determining author's purpose because it can help unlock other subtle messages in the text.

- **Being aware of text language:** This skill was previously discussed in the strategy creating meaningful connections. The literary techniques that an author uses often help a reader visualize ideas and make connections, but they also require a reader to infer the meaning behind the words. For example, a reader needs to think about the meaning the author might be trying to show the reader through descriptions of a character's facial or body expressions, the actions a character takes, or the things a character says. Subtle word play, figurative language, symbolism, and so on require the reader to go beyond the literal and, with the support of connections, deepen and extend the meaning that is being suggested.

- **Recognizing author's biases/views:** Sometimes authors directly communicate their viewpoints; however, their words can also indirectly communicate emotion, bias, attitude, and perspective. Analyzing the examples and evidence cited in text may reveal the writer's bias or value system. The context in which the words are used may deliberately encourage subjective interpretations. Learning to identify the ways an author may manipulate data or expose strong feelings for or against a character, group, or issue supports the ability to infer. Thoughtful readers learn to decipher what is implied or suggested just as well as what is explicitly stated and to separate fact from opinion.

- **Making predictions:** Making predictions is also a skill of inferring. A skillful reader's mind is constantly zooming ahead predicting what may happen next. The subtle clues the author offers trigger predictions about meaning, outcomes, actions of characters, events of a plot, and resolutions of problems. In informational text, features such as bold headings, illustrations, or side notes can be used to predict information that is significant. At the word and sentence level, predictions help in figuring out the word, phrase, or clause (antecedent) to which a pronoun refers and to problem solving unknown words. *Reading on either confirms or changes the predictions.* Predictions are created by integrating the knowledge of the reader with the tacit signals and messages found in text.

- **Determining theme:** The skill of determining theme means a reader must identify the central (and possibly minor) lesson or moral about life, human nature, or the world, that was developed in the selection. A theme emerges after finishing the text, reflecting on the most valuable idea found in the reading, and stating it in a complete sentence. Determining an implied theme requires a reader to think beyond the book as a self-contained experience and reflect deeply on the larger, universal message conveyed. Ideas are discovered through analyzing the characters, their actions, their relationships, issues and conflicts, and outcomes. Searching for evidence of how the message applies in today's world helps themes take on more meaning. For example, after reading *To Kill a Mockingbird* in eighth grade, student discussion generated the following themes such as "Sometimes the people you least expect to step forward will," "People should not be judged by how they look," and "Courage is not always easily noticed."

  Literary devices often provide clues to determining theme. Analyzing the literal and figurative meaning of a character's (or author's) choice of words can help determine the tone and underlying theme the passage addresses. Metaphors and symbols might be used to capture the reader's attention. Also, analyzing the point(s) of conflict may show how the author used tension to reinforce and build themes in the text. Finally, readers often consider the title of a text, along with its introduction and conclusion when determining theme. Determining theme is an intricate skill of the strategy inferring.

- **Drawing conclusions:** The ability to draw conclusions is another important inferring skill. This skill refers to a reader arriving at a logical decision or opinion based on information presented in a text (implied and explicit) combined with the background knowledge and experiences of the reader. Under the strategy inferring, conclusions differ from generalizing the main ideas in text. Inferred conclusions are drawn from judging the relevant facts or evidence presented and coming to an interpretation that was not directly stated. A reader needs to be able to discuss how the implied text information was used to draw his or her conclusion. For example, after reading Barbara Kingsolver's book, *Prodigal Summer,* one might draw the conclusion that, "Barbara Kingsolver wants readers to think about how they interact with the environment." Numerous examples of the consequences that resulted from the various attitudes the characters had about their surroundings and the ways they dealt with the forces of nature could be cited to support this conclusion.

- **Questioning:** A skillful reader generates ongoing questions to facilitate inferring. Questions a reader asks might be: *What conclusion can I draw based on the ideas presented? How do I know the facts are accurate? What opinions were revealed in the selection? Can (a specific statement) be proven true or false? What background information about the author do I need that might help me understand the writer's point of view (Point of reference)? Would another author have a different point of view? What facts were missing? What words and phrases did the author use to present the information? Why did the author write this selection? Where can I find clues about the character's feelings?*

- **Synthesizing text clues and various types of connections:** A reader using this skill fills in details and information about what the writer is implying based on their text connections (text-to-self, text-to-text, or text-to-world). In using this skill, one must have the ability to infer relationships among ideas, characters, actions, and so on and draw a conclusion based on reasoning from personal experiences. Supporting the strategy inferring, synthesizing brings information sources (text and reader) together to create meaning as the text is unfolding.

This Glossary should be a useful reference as you read this book and plan future comprehension lessons. My colleagues and I spent a long time discussing and defining our terms so that, as we worked together, we were speaking the same language. Reading professional literature widely helped us see the variations in different authors' terminology, while examining our own reading behaviors triggered extensive dialogue as we sorted out terms. Through the process of grappling with terminology, the grain size of the points we wanted to make became smaller and finer, thus our thoughts about teaching comprehension became more precise. We cannot be explicit in our teaching until we sharpen our thinking about what we are trying to accomplish and until we can explain the skills and strategies very clearly to the children in our care.

Finally, the interconnections among the Four Powerful Comprehension Strategies and their supporting skills become more obvious in defining each one. This interconnectedness is the reason why Duke and Pearson (2002) tell us that even by learning one strategy deeply and well, a student's comprehension can significantly improve. The interaction of the skills that support the different strategies shows the interrelationships among them and helps students better understand how comprehension works.

Appendix 1

Thinking About How We Use
Strategies to Comprehend

Now, hop into the reading chair! The following activity may help you, as a proficient reader, reflect on all that you do to comprehend text.

ACTIVITY 1: SUMMARIZING

For the first activity, read and then summarize the following paragraph.

Airborne (dietary supplement): Effectiveness studies

Scientific studies supporting Airborne's effectiveness are few in number. The study often referenced in favor of Airborne was sponsored by the Knight-McDowell Labs, manufacturers of Airborne.[1] "GNG Pharmaceutical Services Inc.," claims to have conducted this study with 120 people, and reported that 47% of Airborne recipients showed little or no cold or flu symptoms, whereas only 23% of the recipients of a placebo pill showed equal results.[2] However, in February of 2006, ABC News discovered that GNG Pharmaceutical Services has no official clinic, scientists, or even doctors. In fact the company comprises only two men, who started the company just to perform this study. Because of the bad publicity that this controversy has brought forth, Knight-McDowell Labs has removed all references to the study from their packaging and [W]eb site.[3]

Excerpt of a longer article from: http://en.wikipedia.org/wiki/Airborne_%28dietary_supplement%29

SOURCE: Airborne (dietary supplement). In Wikipedia, the free encyclopedia. Retrieved November 18, 2007, from http://en.wikipedia.org/wiki/Airborne_%28dietary_supplement%29

Below is part of a think-aloud of my *summarizing.* The skills I used for summarizing are in bold print. Compare my think-aloud to the skills you used to summarize the article.

I first notice that this article is from the Web site Wikipedia. I know that articles and definitions on this Web site are contributed by people around the world. The information is then collaboratively edited by the thousands of site visitors (**background knowledge**). This article is from an encyclopedia and after reading the title, I surmise that what I am reading is nonfiction (**identifying genre**) and therefore I expect the text to be filled with factual information. Before I start to read, I ask myself about the credibility of the information (**questioning**). Since the Web site depends on experts in the general public to police the information for correctness, I am wondering who the authors are (**questioning**).

As I begin to read the article, I am trying to grasp how the information is organized (**identifying the type of text structure**). Reading further, I begin to see the author is trying to persuade readers, by citing several studies and data, that Airborne dietary supplement is not effective.

Reading the rest of the paragraph, I note that the first sentence is a general statement. Every other sentence provides very specific information that supports the opening statement. I now recognize that the first sentence of the paragraph is the main idea (**identifying important information**) and the rest is supporting information. This causes me to go back and reread the title of the article. I notice that the title, "Airborne Dietary Supplement: Effectiveness Studies," does not reveal that there is a lack of scientific support for the effectiveness of Airborne (**distinguishing between a topic and main idea**).

I find myself doing more **questioning**: What are the essential points the author is trying to make? I notice there are links, in blue print, embedded in the paragraph (**features of electronic text**). The links are to various studies and sources. When I reference them lower on the page, they appear to be legitimate, and I am wondering if these links will take me to the authors who contributed to the article (**questioning**).

Finally, as I reread the last part of the article (that ABC News exposed GNG Pharmaceutical Services' claims about Airborne, which resulted in the retraction of references to the study from Airborne packaging), my summary of this paragraph is that the manufacturers of Airborne made some strong claims from questionable research that caught up with them (**paraphrasing and generalizing information**).

ACTIVITY 2: CREATING MEANINGFUL CONNECTIONS

All of the skills that support the strategy *creating meaningful connections* occur rapid-fire while reading. Yet, when utilizing this strategy, a reader is deeply engaged with the text. A book that enables a reader to create deep and meaningful connections often leaves an emotional impression that lasts a long time; it is a book that is savored.

As you read the passage below, try to be aware of the skills you are using to help you create meaningful connections with the text. Compare your reading process to the think-aloud that follows.

> The morning sky was featureless, a color like that made on paper from a thin wash of lampblack. Ralph stood stopped in the field, head down, blowing. He was harnessed to a sled load of locus fence rails, and they were heavy as a similar amount of stones. He seemed not to care to draw them one pace farther toward the edge of the creek along which Ruby intended to lay out the snake for a new pasture fence. Ada held the plaited carriage whip, and she popped Ralph's back a time or two with the frizzled end of it to no effect.
>
> —He's a carriage horse, she said to Ruby.
>
> Ruby said, He's a horse.
>
> She went to Ralph's head and took his chin in her hand and looked him in the eye. He put back his ears and showed her a rim of white at the tops of his eyeballs. Ruby pressed her lips to the velvet nose of the horse and then backed off an inch and opened her mouth wide and blew out a deep slow breath into its flanged nostrils. The dispatch sent by such a gesture, she believed, concerned an understanding between them.
>
> —Charles Frazier (1997),
> *Cold Mountain*, p. 186

The author's unusual use of **text language** grabs me immediately. I pause and reread parts of the first sentence, " . . . featureless sky" and "a color like that made on paper by a wash of lampblack." I stop and think about the color of soot that lightly lines one of my candle chimneys (**imaging**) so I can "see" what type of sky the characters are under. I sense that the day is gray, bleak, and cold. At first I wonder if Ralph is blowing from the cold (**questioning**), but as I read further and learn the horse is pulling a sled of locus rails, I now know his heavy breathing is most likely caused by the weight of the load.

When I lived in Ohio, we heated our house by a wood furnace. Locus, an extremely hard wood, was one of the most efficient woods to burn. I also remember how dense and heavy this wood is, so I appreciate the author's comparison of the weight of the rails to a load of stones (**text-to-self connection**).

As I read the description of the character holding the horse's nose and blowing into his nostrils, my mind is taken back to another book I read years ago, *The Horse Whisperer* by Nicholas Evans (**text-to-text connection**). I know a horse whisperer is a person who learns to control horses by gentle body language and voice commands. One of my sisters is a horse trainer, and I remember speaking with her about the book *The Horse Whisperer*. I learned that in building a relationship with a horse, a bond of mutual respect and trust is formed as a human imitates the natural herd instincts of the horse. This is achieved through an approach and retreat series of body language and movements, and by reading the horse's response. By connecting the scene described in this text with what I learned about communicating with horses (**activating**

prior knowledge), I am **synthesizing my connections** with what is happening in this paragraph, and I am **comparing and evaluating** the information in the narrative. As my mind quickly processes these skills, I create a deeper connection to the emotions of the novel's characters and to the setting where this scene is taking place.

ACTIVITY 3: SELF-REGULATING

Can you interpret Shakespeare's sonnet "Unthrifty Loveliness?" If this is a challenge for you to read, you will probably find yourself accessing many of the skills embedded in the strategy *self-regulating* as you attempt to make the sonnet fit together as a coherent whole. Good readers recognize minor comprehension breakdowns before they escalate into major ones and maintain an ongoing, meaningful interaction with the text. Less effective readers, who become aware they cannot make sense of text, often do not know what to do and are quick to give up or rely on outside help. Self-regulating is a strategy at the heart of the comprehension of any reading.

See how frequently you, as a proficient reader, access the skills that support the strategy self-regulating as you read.

William Shakespeare Sonnet 04

Unthrifty loveliness, why dost thou spend

Upon thyself thy beauty's legacy?

Nature's bequest gives nothing but doth lend,

And being frank she lends to those are free.

Then, beauteous niggard, why dost thou abuse

The bounteous largess given thee to give?

Profitless usurer, why dost thou use

So great a sum of sums, yet canst not live?

For having traffic with thyself alone,

Thou of thyself thy sweet self dost deceive.

Then how, when nature calls thee to be gone,

What acceptable audit canst thou leave?

Thy unused beauty must be tomb'd with thee,

Which, used, lives th' executor to be.

My **purpose for reading** is to try to understand what Shakespeare is saying in this sonnet so I can give an interpretation. I am not very familiar with much of Shakespeare's work, or this particular piece, so I know I will need to have a highlighter and be in a quiet spot without distractions as I try to understand what this sonnet is about (**knowing self as a learner**).

I read the first two lines, then slow down (**adjusting reading rate**), and immediately return to the beginning to start again (**rereading**). That didn't help me too much, so I try reading through the whole sonnet once to see if the gist becomes clearer with more text (**reading ahead**). Still confused, I decide to look more closely at key words or phrases (**problem solving words or phrases**). "Unthrifty loveliness;" I know thrifty means frugal or sparse and so *un*thrifty must mean the opposite—this person possesses a great deal of loveliness or beauty." "Why dost thou;" it seems the subject of the poem is being questioned about his or her behavior.

The second line makes no sense so I move on to the third and fourth lines (**reading ahead**). "Nature's bequest gives nothing but doth lend." Now I begin to **predict** that this line might be saying that nature only lends the loveliness referred to in the first line. My prediction seems to be confirmed in line four where the author is saying that one's loveliness is not only a temporary gift, but besides that, the loan is free!

Now I am **questioning** why the author is using so many financial terms such as "unthrifty, bequest, lend." I laboriously continue reading attempting to **clarify, confirm, and revise** the ideas that are beginning to emerge and make more sense.

ACTIVITY 4: INFERRING

Good books arouse emotions and curiosity by omitting just enough information so that a reader creates part of the meaning. The art of *inferring* ignites and excites the reader beyond the words at hand. This strategy and the skills that support it are essential to comprehension.

A sample passage may help explain how these skills support the strategy inferring. As you read the paragraph below, think about the skills you need to help you infer and how you are using them.

> At the hospital the only difference between night and day is the number of nurses on duty. Night shift loses three, half the floor staff. So, the ones on are thinner and move faster; they are also quirkier—women who've made the choice to be awake while everyone else sleeps. Though they have more to do, they sometimes talk longer; occasionally I hear a whole life story: "Married one man I didn't love, another that I did. You want to know the difference in the end? Not much. Swear to God, not much."
>
> —Cammie McGovern (2002),
> *The Art of Seeing*, p. 16

As I read this short paragraph, I immediately start **questioning** why the character is in the hospital. The implicit information in the words, " the only difference between night and day is the number of nurses on duty" makes me **question** if the patient is in a room without windows. The other possibility, in rereading the title of the book is the patient has an eye injury or maybe no sight (**making a prediction**).

The night shift nurses are described as thinner, as moving faster, quirkier, and they talk more. I begin recalling my experience as a hospital patient. I remember how distinctly different the nurses' personalities were (**synthesizing text clues and connections**). I remember having a room outside the nurses' station where there was lots of talking that went on well into the night (**using my background knowledge**).

I am beginning to **draw a conclusion** that the patient is feeling alone and sad. This conclusion seems further confirmed as the patient listens in on a nurse's depressing story about marrying one man she loved, one she didn't, and in the end not finding much difference.

What are some of the skills you found yourself using as you worked through each activity? Because there is such reciprocity among the strategies, you may find there is overlap among them. The fun of this exercise is that it forces us to be conscious and reflective of our own reading processes. Often when we think about what we—as proficient readers—do to make sense of text, it helps us know how to better support the struggling reader.

Appendix 2

Lesson Observation Form

Teaching struggling readers is a challenge. Trusted colleagues, who occasionally take turns observing reading lessons and providing constructive feedback to each other, are extremely valuable and support a genuine professional learning community. This form is designed for note taking while observing a peer teaching a small group reading lesson using the Gradual Release Lesson Design. The bullets are examples of lesson qualities an observer would look for, but they are not intended to serve as a checklist.

(Note: T = teacher; S = student. The circles indicate who has primary responsibility for the step of the lesson.)

Suggested ground rules to establish:

1. Start with the understanding that there is no such thing as a perfect lesson because there are too many complex, unpredictable variables.

2. Time must be set aside to discuss the observation within 24 hours.

3. Observational data will remain confidential.

4. The purpose of the feedback is to provide support to accelerate student success.

5. The observer should share specific examples of what was seen and heard. The observer may also raise questions. Comments should never be judgmental.

6. The teacher may ask for focused feedback on a specific step of the lesson, student, or instructional technique.

7. Both teacher and observer should conclude their discussion with suggestions (at least one) for the next lesson(s).

Lesson Procedures for the Gradual Release of Responsibility

Step 1. An explicit description of the strategy.

Did the teacher

- specifically identify the strategy/skill that will be the teaching point of the lesson?

- clearly explain the importance of the strategy and when it should be used (may also consider a nonexample)?

- keep "teacher talk" to a minimum?

- use language appropriate for the students?

- make an effort to address various learning styles (visual, auditory, and/or verbal cues)?

How did the students respond?

Step 2. Modeling the strategy in action.

Did the teacher

- reinforce key terms of the strategy/skill in context?

- model—show—tell?

- make his or her thinking public (think aloud)?

- make connections to other strategies?

- select examples that clearly support the teaching point?

How did the students respond?

Step 3. Collaborative use of the strategy in action.

Did the teacher

- direct students' practice of the strategy/skill?

- ask guiding questions (explicit and implicit)?

- use high-level/generalizable prompts?

- reinforce the when and why of the strategy/skill?

- invite students into the lesson? ("Let's hear what you think.")

- select the appropriate text for the students and teaching point of the lesson?

- monitor students' understanding of the teaching point?

How did the students respond?

Step 4. Guided practice using the strategy.

Did the teacher

- closely observe/monitor student responses?

- select the appropriate text for the lesson and students' reading level?

- provide opportunities for problem solving and application of the strategy?

- provide positive and corrective feedback? Was it crisp and clear?

- make links from what students know to new learning?

- provide opportunities for students to generate their own questions/ solutions?

How did the students respond?

Step 5. Independent use of the strategy.

T ———(S)

Did the teacher

- provide brief, clear closure to the guided reading lesson—review the teaching point?

- give clear directions for the extension activity?

- incorporate writing into the activity? Use an authentic activity?

- design the follow-up activity so it would provide greater insight in to the students' ability to use the strategy/skill?

- design the activity so that each student is capable of independent success?

How did the students respond?

References

Allington, R. (2001). *What really matters for struggling readers: Designing research-based programs.* Reading, MA: Addison-Wesley Longman.

Anderson, E. (1975). *Thoughts of our times.* Mt Vernon, NY: Peter Pauper Press.

Anderson, N. J. (1991). Individual differences in strategy use in second language reading and testing. *Modern Language Journal, 75,* 450–472.

Anderson, R. C., & Pearson, P. D. (1984). A schematheoretic view of basic processes in reading comprehension. In P. D. Pearson, R. Barr, M. L. Kamil, & P. Mosenthal (Eds.), *Handbook of reading research* (pp. 255–291). New York: Longman.

Beck, I., McKeown, M., Hamilton, R., & Kucan, L. (1997). *Questioning the author: An approach for enhancing student engagement with text.* Newark, DE: International Reading Association.

Bereiter, C. (1995). A dispositional view of transfer. In A. McKeough, J. Lupart, & A. Marini (Eds.), *Teaching for transfer: Fostering generalization in learning* (pp. 21–34). Mahwah, NJ: Lawrence Erlbaum.

Bigge, M., & Shermis, S. (1999). *Learning theories for teachers.* New York: Longman.

Bransford, J., Brown, A., & Cocking, R. (Eds.). (2000). *How people learn: Brain, mind, experience, and school* (Expanded ed.). Committees on Developments in the Science of Learning and Committee on Learning Research and Educational Practice, Commission on Behavioral and Social Sciences and Education, National Research Council. Washington: DC: National Academies Press.

Bransford, J., & Swartz, D. L. (1999). Rethinking transfer: A simple proposal with multiple implications. In A. Iran-Nejad & P. D. Pearson (Eds.), *Review of educational research* (Vol. 24). Washington, DC: American Educational Research Association.

Cooper, J. D., Pikulski, J., Au, K., Calderon, M., & Comas, J. (1997). *Invitations to literacy.* Boston: Houghton Mifflin.

Dole, J. (2000). Explicit and implicit instruction in comprehension. In B. M. Taylor, M. E. Graves, & P. Van Den Broek (Eds.), *Reading for meaning: Fostering comprehension in the middle grades* (pp. 52–69). Newark, DE: International Reading Association.

Dole, J. A., Duffy, G. G., Roehler, L. R., & Pearson, P. D. (1991). Moving from the old to the new: Research on reading comprehension. *Review of Educational Research, 61,* 239–264.

Dorn, L., & Soffos, C. (2005). *Teaching for deep comprehension: A reading workshop approach.* Portland, ME: Stenhouse.

Drew, E. (1926). *The modern novel.* Orlando, FL: Harcourt, Brace.

Duke, N., & Pearson, P. D. (2002). *Effective practices for developing reading comprehension.* In A. E. Farstrup & S. J. Samuels (Eds.), *What research has to say about reading instruction* (3rd ed., pp. 205–242). Newark, DE: International Reading Association.

Duke, N., Purcell-Gates, V., Hall, L., & Tower, C. (2006, December/2007, January). Authentic literacy activities for developing comprehension and writing. *The Reading Teacher, 60* (4), 344–355.

Durkin, D. (1978–1979). What classroom observations reveal about reading comprehension instruction. *Reading Research Quarterly, 14* (4), 481–533.

Durkin, D. (1993). *Teaching them to read* (6th ed.). Needham, MA: Allyn & Bacon.

El-Dinary, P. (2002). Challenges of implementing transactional strategies instruction for reading comprehension. In C. Block & M. Pressley (Eds.), *Comprehension instruction* (pp. 201–215). New York: Guilford Press.

Erickson, H. L. (2002). *Concept-based curriculum and instruction: Teaching beyond the facts.* Thousand Oaks, CA: Corwin Press.

Erickson, H. L. (2007). *Concept-based curriculum and instruction for the thinking classroom.* Thousand Oaks, CA: Corwin Press.

Flood, J., & Lapp, D. (1991). *Reading Comprehension Instruction.* In J. Flood, J. Jensen, D. Lapp, and J. Squire (Eds). *Handbook of research on teaching the English language arts* (pp. 732–742). New York: MacMillan Publishing Company.

Fountas, I. C., & Pinnell, G. S. (2001). *Guiding readers and writers grades 3–6: Teaching comprehension, genre, and content literacy.* Portsmouth, NH: Heinemann.

Frazier, C. (1997). *Cold mountain.* New York: Atlantic Monthly Press.

Fry, R. (1994). *Improve your reading* (2nd ed.). Franklin Lakes, NJ: Career Press.

Gambrell, L., & Koskinen, P. (2002). *Imagery: A strategy for enhancing comprehension.* In C. C. Block & M. Pressley (Eds.), *Comprehension instruction: Research-based best practices* (pp. 305–318). New York: Guilford Press.

Goodman, K. (1986). *What's whole in whole language.* Portsmouth, NH: Heinemann Educational Books.

Harris, T., & Hodges, R. (1995). *The literacy dictionary: The vocabulary of reading and writing.* Newark, DE: International Reading Association.

Harvey, S., & Goudvis, A. (2000). *Strategies that work: Teaching comprehension to enhance understanding.* York, ME: Stenhouse.

Hill, H. (2001). Policy is not enough: Language and the interpretation of state standards. *American Educational Research Journal, 38*(2), 289–318.

International Reading Association. (2003). *Focus on reading comprehension: IRA programs and resources.* Retrieved May 2003, from http://www.reading.org/resources/issues/focus_comprehension.html

Irwin, J. (1989). *Teaching reading comprehension processes* (2nd ed.). Englewood Cliffs, NJ: Prentice Hall.

Iser, W. (1978). *The act of reading: A theory of aesthetic response.* Baltimore, MD: Johns Hopkins University Press.

Ivey, G., & Fisher, D. (2007). *Creating literacy-rich schools for adolescents.* Alexandria, VA: Association for Supervision and Curriculum Development.

James, M. (2006). Teaching for transfer in ELT. *English Language Teaching, 60*(2), 151–159.

Jitendra, A., Hoppes, M., & Xin-Ping, Y. (2000). Enhancing main idea comprehension for students with learning problems: The role of a summarization strategy and self-monitoring instruction. *Journal of Special Education, 34* (3), 127–139.

Keene, E., & Zimmermann, S. (1997). *Mosaic of thought: Teaching comprehension in a reader's workshop.* Portsmouth, NH: Heinemann.

Kingsolver, B. (1995). Jabberwocky. In *High tide in Tucson: Essays from now or never* (pp. 222–235). New York: HarperCollins.

Kong, A. (2002). *Scaffolding in a learning community of practice: A case study of a gradual release of responsibility from the teacher to the students.* Paper presented at the Annual Meeting of the International Reading Association, San Francisco, April 28–May 2, 2002.

Livingston, J. (1997). *Metacognition: An overview.* Retrieved October 2002, from http://www.gse.buffalo.edu/fas/shuell/CEP564/Metacog.htm

Manning, M. (2002). *Teaching pre K–8: Self-monitoring reading.* Retrieved May 2008, from http://www.findarticles.com/p/articles/mi_qa3666/is_200201/ai_n9065913/print

McEwan, E. (2004). *7 strategies of highly effective readers.* Thousand Oaks, CA: Corwin Press.

McGovern, C. (2002). *The art of seeing.* New York: Scribner.

McKeough, A., Lupart, J., & Marini, A. (1995). *Teaching for transfer: Fostering generalization in learning.* Mahwah, NJ: Lawrence Erlbaum.

Meyer, D. (1993). What is scaffolded instruction? Definitions, distinguishing features, misnomers. In D. J. Leu & C. K. Kinzer (Eds.), *Examining central issues in literacy research, theory, and practice: Forty-second yearbook of the National Reading Conference* (pp. 41–53). Washington, DC: National Reading Conference.

Moser, G., & Morrison, T. (1998). Increasing students' achievement and interest in reading. *Reading Horizons, 3,* 233–245.

National Institute of Child Health and Human Development. (2000). Report of the national reading panel. *Teaching children to read: An evidence-based assessment of the scientific research literature on reading and its implications for reading instruction.* NIH Publication No. 00-4769. Washington, DC: U.S. Government Printing Office.

Oczkus, L. (2004). *Super 6 comprehension strategies.* Norwood, MA: Christopher-Gordon.

Pearson, P. D., & Gallagher, M. (1983). The instruction of reading comprehension. *Contemporary Educational Psychology, 8,* 317–344.

Pearson, P. D., & Johnson, D. (1978). *Teaching reading comprehension.* New York: Holt, Rinehart & Winston.

Pearson, P. D., Roehler, L., Dole, J., & Duffy, G. (1992). Developing expertise in reading comprehension. In S. J. Samuels & A. E. Farstrup (Eds.), *What research has to say about reading instruction* (2nd ed., pp. 145–199). Newark, DE: International Reading Association.

Perkins, D. N., & Salomon, G. (1988). Teaching for transfer. *Educational Leadership, 46* (1), 22–32.

Probst, R. (2004). *Response and analysis: Teaching literature in secondary school* (2nd ed.). Portsmouth, NH: Heinemann.

RAND Reading Study Group (RRSG). (2002). *Reading for understanding: Toward an R&D program in reading comprehension.* Washington, DC: RAND Corporation.

Robb, L. (2000). *Teaching reading in the middle school.* New York: Scholastic.

Rosenblatt, L. M. (1978). *The reader, the text, the poem: The transactional theory of the literary work.* Carbondale: Southern Illinois University Press.

Rumelhart, D. E. (1980). Schemata: The building blocks of cognition. In R. J. Spiro, B. C. Bruce, & W. F. Brewer (Eds.), *Theoretical issues in reading comprehension* (pp. 33–58). Hillsdale, NJ: Lawrence Erlbaum.

Sinatra, G. M., Brown, K. J., & Reynolds, R. E. (2002). Implications of cognitive resource allocation for comprehension strategy instruction. In C. Block & M. Pressley (Eds.), *Comprehension instruction* (pp. 62–76). New York: Guilford Press.

Vygotsky, L. S. (1978). *Mind in society: The development of higher psychological processes* (M. Cole, V. John-Steiner, S. Scribner, & E. Souberman, Eds. & Trans.). Cambridge, MA: Harvard University Press.

Wood, D. (1998). *How children think and learn* (2nd ed.). Malden, MA: Blackwell.

Zwiers, J. (2004) *Building reading comprehension habits in grades 6–12: A toolkit of classroom activities.* Newark, DE: International Reading Association.

Index

CORWIN PRESS

The Corwin Press logo—a raven striding across an open book—represents the union of courage and learning. Corwin Press is committed to improving education for all learners by publishing books and other professional development resources for those serving the field of PreK–12 education. By providing practical, hands-on materials, Corwin Press continues to carry out the promise of its motto: **"Helping Educators Do Their Work Better."**

The mission of the International Reading Association is to promote reading by continuously advancing the quality of literacy instruction and research worldwide.